With Christian Love

More
Understanding the New Age

& Best wishes

Discerning Antichrist
and the Occult Revival

Roy Livesey

8 Jan 94

New Wine Press

New Wine Press
P.O. Box 17
Chichester PO20 6YB
England

All quotations are from the Authorised Version of The Bible.

British Library Cataloguing in Publication Data
Livesey, Roy
  More understanding the new age
  1. Antichrist
  I. Title
  236

ISBN 0-947852-62-X

Contents

1

The New Age

In the first edition of Understanding the New Age I wrote that it would not be in Satan's interests that Bible-believing Christians should be aware of the New Age movement. I wrote that it was a measure of his achievement, in Britain at least, and many other countries excluding the United States, that vast numbers have never heard the name "New Age," let alone have any understanding of what is happening in the spiritual dimension of the occult realm.

Since then two things have happened. *First,* we have seen more Christian books in Britain on this subject since my own books were written. *Second,* it has become more clear to me just how significant Rome and the Ecumenical movement in the New Age picture are. Rome is very significant.

The many groups coming together in the New Age would in the natural world seem to have little in common. As Christians we fellowship with people where in the normal way there would be no common interest or social point of contact. Similarly when I was involved with New Age groups, and later on involved more directly in the occult, my colleagues were mostly those with whom there would otherwise be little in common.

Eastern mysticism has been traditionally reclusive - something to enjoy in private. If you were meditating in a Himalayan cave it would only hinder the purpose to join a group for the exercise! When it came to sects there would be power in a group, but in the East there would be an exclusivity and a marked absence of public relations and display. Today in the West we are being evangelised. Puny-looking youngsters with shaved heads can occasionally be seen banging their drums and dancing through the shopping precinct of the town nearest their Hindu Colony. Transcendental Meditation has arrived from the East, and it is big business. The Eastern religions are coming out into the open. The freedom they enjoy in the West is only *one* reason for this. At grass roots level, Rome does not meet them. Yet it has fostered the globalism, the "unity." Indeed in these days the world's religious leaders are making tracks to Rome.

If you look for a single human organising principle behind what is going on in every area of the world you won't find one! The cohesion of all that can be identified is such that the central control has to be identified as being in the spiritual realm. The pieces of the jig-saw are falling together. It is all according to God's Word and fore-knowledge.

As the Eastern religions have come out into the open they have found others with a great deal in common. On the religious front the Church of Rome is moving towards ecumenism with Eastern Religions and New Age groups, as well as with Christian denominations. Our Western society generally has moved on in the ways of the occult. This has all accelerated in the past twenty-five years, and on the occult front people have moved on from the drug culture to the powerful quickly-effective mind control techniques such as biofeedback to reach 'high levels of consciousness.' I reached the point where I believed in reincarnation and where I was praying to Sai Baba, an incarnate Indian god. Through drugs it is possible to reach states of consciousness still unknown to many in the West; from there progress can be made. Once we step into the occult realm we are set to become more and more blinded to the truth of God's Word, and Satan is given the opportunity to make his hold stronger.

2

Unity in a Counterfeit Spirit

As a Christian I attended a "Mind, Body, Spirit" festival. Although staged in a very small town, the festival housed over eighty stands and displays.

What a mixture of people I found in that place, people so different in every way, yet to the discerning it could be seen that they had much in common. There was an evident unity of spirit and the most significant differences among the stall holders could best be seen in terms of where they each were along the New Age road and in the direction of what many there would call "the higher levels of consciousness."

That state may most usefully be explained as something like a trance state in which normal functions may be performed.

People who were steeped in the occult, and who would be attracted to such a place, moved about the stalls alongside the range of people who had seen the press advertising. Men, women and children who were passing by wandered in from the street to see what it was all about. There was something for everyone throughout the day with mediumship demonstrations and Eastern religious dancing with the public invited up to the platform to join in.

Stalls included several who offered fortune telling and tarot reading. Another man had a big display of crystals. "Just look upon all the crystals and let your hand go towards the one that first attracts you. That's *your* crystal. Pick it up and put it against your body where you have a complaint, or just move it intuitively to one part of your body," he told me. "There's healing with crystals, you know." Other stalls had objects to hang in windows or to put on the sideboard - glass rainbows, little owls, occultic crosses, to mention a few. Next door to the Campaign for Nuclear Disarmament (CND) stall manned by college students in patched-up jeans there was a smart lady in a two-piece suit selling what looked like jam; she said she was there to "hold the fort" on the Vegan table. From the conversation we had this particular lady had long been a vegetarian for what were very plausible reaons, but now

3

without realising it, she was being drawn into something much more subtle. Every stall in that festival was a part of the New Age movement. Perhaps even the Nuclear Disarmament campaigners there didn't know it. I was once a member of CND myself. I joined because I believed I was joining something that would be positive, actually *do* something and be effective, unlike the political groups I had been involved with and even led. Of course I had no idea that what I was joining was a part of the New Age movement, just as much as the psychic and spiritual counterfeit groups that I was later to get involved with.

The festival had an enormous number of spiritually powerful occultists of one sort and another. Some represented the Eastern religions. There were psychic healers. It was possible to pay and get a biorhythm chart, another deception increasingly looked at by alternative medical practitioners. It holds that there are three body cycles (physical - twenty-three days; emotional - twenty-eight days and intellectual - thirty-three days) running from birth to death. The idea is to avoid stressful occasions and potential illness on particular days. Its charts, like those in astrology, are for the curious and seem to have no basis in science. Rather the information is provided by demons in order to deceive. Like the rest of the New Age the results come from a focus on the creation instead of upon the Creator.

Focusing on Creation; Not the Creator

Every group in that festival was focusing on the creation just as Eve did in the Garden of Eden. It would have been far better for Eve if she had focused on the Creator and what He had said, but instead she looked at all the trees

4

bearing fruit in the garden. She wanted to be *"as gods"* (Genesis 3:5) in the way the serpent had described the situation, and as she looked at the tree of knowledge with her natural eyes she must have seen that it was growing in the same ground as the tree of life. How *could* it be different, she might have thought, when both were coming out of the same place - the ground? She fell into Satan's trap and took her eyes off the Creator.

At the festival there were broadly two groups. One group comprised people who sought to *protect* the creation, and of course there is nothing basically wrong in that. Indeed our creation does need to be respected and looked after, but this New Age group is especially zealous in its campaigning and its efforts. It is a group with very many sincere people with a genuine care in their hearts, whether for the seals that are to be protected or for the food value of what is served up in the grocery store; whether for the forests or for the starving in India, or for our survival through banning the bomb or getting missiles out of Britain. Ever since Adam, natural man has focused upon himself and the creation of which he is part (Romans 1:17-32). Satan is the god of this world and he has seen to it that it has been so (2 Corinthians 4:3-4). The last thing he has wanted is a focus upon the Creator - Jesus. However nearly 2,000 years after the birth of Jesus Christ and nearly 6,000 years since Adam was created, the picture of our world system, readily available through travel, literature and media communication is becoming very clear.

The second group of New Agers at the festival sought to *understand* the creation. Those who are plumbing the depths for an understanding of the creation, whether by divining for water or for anything else, whether by clairvoyance or ESP power, or whether by probing or correcting the so-called ley-lines or energy forces under the earth, have gone a long way along the road of deception. Whether they came to this place via a focus on the protection of the creation, or more directly through a curiosity with the occult or a desire for its power, they find

5

themselves in the vanguard of the movement. At first not all at a festival will understand the ways of this second group. Yet they will be recognised by all who are new to the scene as people with a common focus.

New Agers do *care* about the creation. They are not generally apathetic. They may not all have a job or generally do conventional things, but then in common with Christians, they look at the materialism and selfishness of the world and think: "What a mess!" Often the New Ager will step *back* from all this and then step *out* of the conventional world situation. The New Ager's cause becomes his religion, and that devotion and the unity with others equally committed makes a powerful tool in Satan's hands; it straddles politics and international borders. The unity, power and strength grows. It is the New Age movement.

The New Age Rainbow

The wider movement was clearly to be understood from my visit to that small-town festival. The event was a milestone on the road to the fuller understanding since first hearing the expression "New Age." That was in California in January 1984. As watchmen we do need to keep an eye on the United States. For me this understanding came from visits there as a Christian, and back in 1984 a Christian friend pointed out a rainbow sign in the window of an automobile. "That's a New Age rainbow," he told me. From that day I noticed the rainbows, perhaps more in evidence then than they are today, and I became alert to the New Age in its various concepts.

You couldn't miss the rainbow symbol, displayed in one way or another on so many of the stalls at the festival. The rainbow is a prominent symbol used by the New Age movement. Indeed it is used as a hypnotic device. They call it the "International Sign of Peace." What a clever choice for a symbol! Once again Satan begins with something good and comes up with a *symbol* to match the *real* rainbow put into the sky as a sign of God's everlasting covenant after the flood.

Greenpeace is one growing ecology movement now rivalling CND for membership growth. It was a tragedy that the Greenpeace ship "Rainbow Warrior" was sunk off New Zealand. In introducing the successes in its battle for the environment Greenpeace, in a booklet I acquired at the festival, put its position in terms used by the old American Indians and taken on board by Greenpeace in the New Age: When the Earth is sick and the animals have disappeared, there will come a tribe of peoples from all creeds, colours and cultures who believe in deeds not words and who will restore the Earth to its former beauty. This tribe they tell us will be called the 'Warriors of the Rainbow.' That was certainly prophetic and we have that "tribe" today. Those Indian words well describe the New Age movement and its focus on the creation.

The truth is to be found in God's word and not in the fables of American Indians. Isaiah writes that *"the heavens shall vanish away like smoke, and the earth shall wax old like a garment, and they that dwell therein shall die in like manner"* (Isaiah 51:6). The earth will not be restored to its former beauty, but, with wonderful expectation Isaiah continues, *"my salvation shall be for ever."* New Agers are missing the eternal life with the Lord in heaven, as they keep their eyes set on the earth and the creation all about them.

The New Age Elite — In Touch With The Coming Christ!

There are many today who believe they hear a "Christ" speak of his coming. Often demons speak with an audible voice. It still may be a comparatively rare phenomenon, yet the numbers who choose not to take the "narrow road" of

7

Scripture will be large (Matthew 7:14). They come from East and West.

There are countless aspects to the deception. We can trace the New Age in the West back to the religions of the East, and beyond that back to Babylon. It advanced from there spawning its many branches. Accordingly it is vast and complex today.

There is a narrow identifiable MOVEMENT and so I don't dispute with those who give a definition of the New Age that is less comprehensive than my own. There are those who recognise they are New Agers. They follow the teachings of leaders like Benjamin Creme, Alice Bailey, Annie Besant, and further back still, Helena Blavatsky, who came from India and is credited with bringing New Age philosophy with her. That was the start of the Theosophical Society more than 100 years ago.

These are all important leaders who, whilst being dreadfully deceived, we do well to take seriously today. Their relevance is that these - and many more - are in the West. Their followers number in the multi-millions and they are invoking the return of "Christ." But are they really being prepared to welcome the one who will be a future Antichrist? These New Agers with their beliefs in karma, reincarnation, evolution, and all the rest from the East, look forward to what advanced New Agers know as a Quantum Leap, a sudden evolution of all mankind to a "new consciousness." At least, they would add, that's for all who would remain on earth. It will be a time, they teach, when Christians will disappear from earth to improve their ways before reincarnating once again to improve their karma. They look for a time of "leap" or transition from the Age of Pisces to the Age of Aquarius. They believe in *physical* evolution, and this is their *metaphysical* or spiritual evolution. They are New Agers because they look for a New Age on earth soon - a time of peace and prosperity. Their leaders speak of the "Third Wave" or the

8

"Aquarian Age." Christians have accepted their phrase, "the Aquarian Conspiracy." As Christians our outlook is different. We look forward to seeing the Lord. We believe we may be called to face persecution before that time (2 Timothy 3: 12), but nevertheless we are to encourage one another with the certainty of the wonderful prospect of His coming (1 Thessalonians 4:18).

The "Third Wave"

The "Third Wave" describes one very popular wing of New Age thought. The expression was coined in the United States and it offers what is believed to be a way out of today's despair giving a so-called optimistic look at what are seen as our new potentials. The "Third Wave" view, much promoted both innocently and deliberately in literature, is that the human story is not one that is ending but one that is just beginning. As Christians we can know that these New Agers are fairly accurately observing the signs of the times and like them we know that the changes we see today are not independent of one another. These New Age people know that the global energy crisis, the spread of the cults, the growth of TV including cable TV, and a host of other events *seem* isolated one from another, but they know they are not. It is here that the common ground with the Christian ends.

Having observed the signs of the times, the New Agers looking for the Third Wave see the future as one with the deepest social upheaval and restructuring of all time resulting in the building of what is seen as a new civilization. It is that new civilization that gives meaning to the use of the expression "Third Wave." It provides the reasoning and perhaps the excuse for the extraordinary changes that are forseen. And they aim some of these at Christians, who they believe need changing! The First Wave is seen as the agricultural revolution and the Second Wave as the rise of industrial civilization. They see renewable energy sources and a new way of life based on new methods of production that will make most assembly lines look obsolete. This new way of life will, they believe, be one based upon a new code of behaviour. As in all New Age perspectives we are treated to new jargon; the idea of an "electronic cottage" describes many homes even today. The New Agers can know, as Christians know, that this trend is set to increase. The "Third Wave" perspective is essentially a political one but it has little regard for the politics of our recognised leaders. They will meet those who have the occult-based perspective of the Aquarian conspirators somewhere along the line, but this far the "Third Wave" people see the new civilization simply as one that challenges the old on its own terms. They see a new code of behaviour beyond the present one governed by energy, money and power. It will be one that sets aside the existing bureaucraciès and reduces the role of individual governments. It is in recognition of the growth of this sort of thinking, widespread but unrecognised by most, that the Christian reply must be a clear and persistent one. New Agers, both in the "Third Wave" and in the "Aquarian Conspiracy" looked at later in this chapter, are preparing for the future. They know nothing of a future in the presence of the Lord Jesus Christ, or of one in hell eternally separated from Him (John 3:36).

Christians do well to take care in identifying with New Age efforts lest, unequally yoked, they march with them into *their* perspective of the future. The Bible can provide the only discernment and it presents no such attractive future. Luke wrote:

And when ye see the south wind blow, ye say, There will be heat; and it cometh to pass.

Ye hypocrites, ye can discern the face of the sky and of the earth; but how is it that ye do not discern this time?

(Luke 12:55-56)

That scripture has been relevant for 2000 years. However the world is made a small place today through control and communication, the means to which rest in relatively few hands. The inquisition of the sixteenth century or the United States Declaration of Independence were local revolutions, significant in different ways in their day. Today we have the fact of a global scenario - a movement to World Government, yet the truth is in Scripture and in its warnings. The signs change but the Bible does not (Matthew 24:35; 1 Peter 1:25).

The Third Wave is well described in a best-selling book of that name written by Alvin Toffler in 1980. It is an important book for it summarises so well Man's ever-optimistic view of the world and his ability to weigh up the situation and attempt to put things right. Seeing the two spiritual realms with similar scorn he misses what the Bible has to offer. However, not focusing on the occult realm, he summarises the New Age of Man as he focuses on himself, and on the creation we too readily see as being the answer. I could identify with that position. It was a position I once took, before being led into the occult realm, whilst I was still successfully achieving my own ends in business and industry; I can imagine Satan had no need of me any deeper into his realm while I continued to serve his purposes in that way. I can understand the worldwide acclaim the book received from the international press including The Washington Post, Le Figaro, The Guardian, Neue Züricher Zeitung, Toronto Globe and Mail, Business Week, Vogue, Financial World, and Cosmopolitan. Alas, even the "Church Times" described the book as a superb statement. This Church of England newspaper went as far as to say that no other book would make such a useful resource for any Christian willing to learn!

New Agers focus wherever they are directed, but all seem agreed they are entering an exciting new age, one full of promise. Focusing on the universe too, the belief is in the end of the old Age of Pisces. They are all set to enter the New Age of Aquarius.

11

The Aquarian Conspiracy

As we look still further for good definitions of the New Age movement to serve as a basis for the depth and breadth of the later chapters, it is natural to go to "The Aquarian Conspiracy" by Marilyn Ferguson. Like Toffler's book it is dated 1980. Like Toffler's book also it is comprehensive. "The Third Wave" looked at the way Man is seeking to *protect* the creation. Marilyn Ferguson's book looks from the New Ager's point of view at Man seeking to *understand* the creation. Toffler's book looked at what Man can do without too much evident supernatural assistance; Marilyn Ferguson takes a view based on much plucking from the tree of knowledge.

Thus once again a much respected New Ager purports to bring optimism and good news:

....that we are in the midst of a knowledge revolution that shows signs of breakthrough: that researchers in the human sciences are moving independently in converging lines towards common targets; that they are discarding traditional models of the cosmos and ourselves - of the nature of nature and the nature of human nature - and reaching for new ones; that they have been spurred on by recent work on the brain hemispheres, on molecular biology and biochemistry, on the genetic code, on primatology and ethnology, on biofeedback and altered states of consciousness, on medicine and psychotherapies, on archaeology and astronomy, on the evolutionary process, on the structure of language and the nature of meaning, of leadership and power, and on the governance of peoples and nations. Thus the startling fact is that for the first time an American renaissance is taking place in all disciplines, breaking the boundaries between them, transforming them at their farthest reaches - where they all converge. *

What it really amounted to was that Marilyn Ferguson was finding, as a "searcher"/researcher, that not only

* "The Aquarian Conspiracy" by Marilyn Ferguson (Paladin: Granada - 1984) Foreword by Max Lerner.

12

were people demonstrating abilities that defied previous scientific understanding, but also that science was changing its position too. As she put it:

"Science, in its objective fashion, was generating surprising data about human nature and the nature of reality...."

New Agers and Occult Power

What Marilyn Ferguson had discovered was the occult psychic dimension, the dimension that more and more scientists are moving into. When I was training to be a psychic healer during my time as a "searcher" into the occult realm one of my teachers, an internationally-known "healer", told of how he was able to destroy cancer cells by the power of his mind. He told of the occasion he did this under close scientific supervision in a well-equipped laboratory. The professor in charge of the operation was a physicist of unquestioned reputation, but whatever his purpose, in innocent ignorance or with full understanding, there is no way a scientist or anyone else can involve himself with the powers of darkness without being influenced by them. In the medical field I heard of one psychiatrist who was converted to an Eastern religion in the course of counselling a patient. Turning to medical science, one Christian doctor has written to me:

While the medical profession today tries to convince itself that there is a very strong scientific basis for all that we do ... When you begin to explore medicine from a totally scientific viewpoint you find vast, and I mean literally vast, areas of physiology and biochemistry which are not understood at all and much of that which is supposedly understood is at best theory which as we all know constantly changes. Nowhere is this more than in the area of neuro-physiology and neuro-biochemistry which clearly have direct bearing on the psyche. *

With science so uncertain, with so many subjects in these

---

* "Understanding Alternative Medicine" by Roy Livesey (New Wine Press) - 1988.

days, as we shall see later able to perform super-human functions under the influence of demons, and with more and more scientists being drawn into the supernatural, is it surprising that any New Age "searcher"/researcher is going to make some extraordinary discoveries? Yet it is only when we know the Lord Jesus Christ that we can know the truth that sets us free (John 14:6; John 8:36).

2

History of The New Age

The foundation for today's New Age movement is Hinduism. Two things make Hinduism deserving of at least a short section in any book on the New Age:

1. Hinduism can accommodate any *religion* but it cannot accommodate Biblical Christianity.
2. The occult and New Age deceptions that we look at in this book are substantially rooted in Hinduism.

The two statements above go easily together. I believe they are the key to an understanding of Hinduism and its significance in the end-time scenario.

Hinduism - The Predominant World View in the West

At the intellectual level the religion is full of contradiction when viewed from a Western perspective. Sai Baba, perhaps the most powerful psychic in the world today, is styled by his followers as god, yet he acknowledges we are all gods. In puja rooms all over the world statues of Sai Baba are brought by his followers to be blessed by the manifestation of his sacred ash upon them. He is happy for statues of Jesus Christ to be taken to those same puja rooms to be blessed in a similar way. Satan and his demons are in control of the situation and the lie which they promote, and which runs through the Hindu rationale, is that God is part of His own creation.

This is often expressed in the term - "all is one". All is god, and the whole creation hangs together by a "force". Hindu mystics and gurus have for long tuned into this force and become aware of their 'godhood' and 'oneness' with the creation. Hinduism is significant in the New Age context because this monistic ("all is one") view of reality has progressively and quickly displaced Christianity as the world view predominant in the West. This is manifestly true when we look at alternative medicine and the branches of psychology at work in that and other areas, in science, in sociology and in eduaction. Evolution, reincarnation and all the other aspects essential to Hinduism are found in the Religious Education taught in Western schools, where the Bible is an unknown book to vast numbers of youngsters.

The Hindu world-view is significant throughout the United Nations' agencies and even though the U.N. is vulnerable to the influence of Jesuitry or Illuminati-type groups*, we can be sure there is no clash between its management and the philosophy.

"The whole world lieth in wickedness," as we read in 1 John 5:19, and through the stepping up of occult influence among the secret groups they are all being brought more squarely into the New Age. Ecumenism is continuing throughout all religions and not only among professing Christians. The Jesuits and the upper echelons of the Church of Rome are into the occult mysteries so familiar to the god-men of the East. The Dalai Lama, a *Buddhist* spiritual leader became president of the 1979 World *Hindu* Conference. I can foresee no conflict between the Church of Rome and the followers of the Hindu religion. The ground is being well prepared. The conversion of the Western world to Hinduism, so well founded on the occult philosophy now so familiar in the West, has involved many years of subtle promotion.

The Theosophical Society after its launch in 1875 combined the mysticism of Egypt and gnosticism, itself a combination of what seemed the most attractive teachings of ancient

* These influences are looked at in some detail in "Understanding the New Age - World Government and World Religion" (New Wine Press - 1989). This book shows the effects of New Age influence within the mostly unrecognised power groups working for one-world government and one-world religion.

Greece, Judaism, the Eastern religions and Christianity. We only have to look around us to know the Theosophist "Plan" is working out. Let us look at the evidence.

Yoga classes are held everywhere in the West, and Yoga is Hindu. Self-realisation is its aim. Although it's not taught in the first course of lessons, and certainly even some teachers may not know it, the aim is to realise that we are gods. The class sits quietly in its yoga positions. There is a stillness and a peace. There is a oneness. There comes a realisation that "all is one". Every yoga teacher is a Hindu missionary.

Then there is a renewed interest in Sanskrit literature. The literature consists largely of hymns of praise and prayer, with sacrificial formulas and incantations as repeated by the priests. The Sanskrit literature is from India; it is in the sacred and ancient language of the Hindus.

Meditation of one sort and another, Transcendental Meditation, hypnosis and every variation can be found; they are really all the same and known to the yogis and gurus of the East for thousands of years. Their purpose in Satan's scheme is to bring a unity between Man and God - the abstract Hindu god who is really anybody and everybody. Yoga is a Hindi word which comes from the Sanskrit "yo" and "ga" - Man and God. The aim is for a unity such as is found by a drop of water when it falls into the sea. You can't find that drop of water anywhere. You believe you have become like God, but in fact you have lost your identity. The serpent lied when he encouraged Eve to question God and told her she would never die. Satan is the liar in Hinduism too; there is no prospect of becoming like God, identity is lost. Soon everything can be lost if the Hindu way is followed.

Hinduism is the basis of so many cults. Cults draw heavily on Hindu philosophy and teaching. The Vedas are the source of much hidden knowledge passed down through the generations to those in the high caste. The language is Sanskrit and the literature comprises the ancient knowledge seen in Babylon and which Eve had chosen by her disobedience. The answer is not in the spirituality of the Sanskrit language and Hindu philosophy.

My expectation as a Christian has nothing in common with

17

Hinduism. I do not look forward any more to a reincarnation after death. Sai Baba, the god-man to whom I at one time prayed, is no answer for the souls who visit his ashram in their tens of thousands. He is a man deceived and possessed, perhaps like no other man alive today; he is a Hindu in India. My expectation is not of a merger with God to be all-one with Him. The promise that I have is that I shall see Him face to face (Revelation 22: 4). The distinction between me, a creature, and God my creator will always remain. I shall never become God. I shall never become equal to God. I shall never merge in Him. *There* lies the difference between Hinduism and Christianity.

What else does Hinduism teach? First there is reincarnation, the idea that after death we return to earth with another life. Hinduism teaches "You will never die. You will become God." The cruel lie of the serpent in Genesis 3:4 operates. Then there is karma, the idea that conditions in the next life are determined by those in the present one. What little incentive there is for the people to leave the streets of Calcutta even if they could. To help them would only serve to influence their karma for the next life. What we find among the most popular beliefs in the West in these days are little different.

Hinduism can accommodate all religions. Mother Teresa's staff encourage the dying to pray to their own god. The counterfeit Church of Rome, to which she belongs, brings these religions together in our day. In India Mother Teresa ministers to Hindus. The foundations for world religion are being laid, and at gatherings such as we saw at Assisi in 1986, it is the Hindus who are most readily accomodated.

The Theosophical Society

Out of Hinduism, the Theosophical Society was born.

It has been said that the New Age Movement in modern times can be traced back to 1875. This was a significant time which saw the beginning of the Theosophical Society. Helena Blavatsky wrote in that year that the Christians and scientists must be made to respect their Indian betters. She told us that the wisdom of India, her philosophy and achievement, had to be made known in Europe and America and the English made to respect the natives of India and Tibet more than they did.

The Theosophical Society fronts today connect closely at many points with the activities of the United Nations* but our main purpose is to understand its occult nature.

Mental telepathy is not scientific. It is another branch of the occult and Madame Blavatsky worked in "telepathic" communication with the "Masters" who guided her. She didn't recognise the significance of the demonic source of supernatural information.

The Theosophists held that these "Masters" were higher spirit beings. Like the Hindus, the Theosophists accommodated all religions seeing the common truths that transcended the differences. As usual the odd one out was the Christian Bible believer. Christianity came under attack on the philosophical level through the Theosophical Society. Blavatsky's successor was Annie Besant, and eventually the mantle fell to Alice Bailey.

Alice Bailey and her Spirit Guide "The Tibetan" give us Holistic Health and Spiritual Music

It was in 1975, after Mrs Bailey had died, that on her say-so the time had come to launch the message. She declared Holistic Health to be part of that message. 1976 saw the formalised attitude of the United Nations, through the World Health Organisation (WHO), towards traditional (or alternative) medicine. Can it be a coincidence that in the same year the World Council of Churches (WCC) shifted its attention too and began sponsoring workshops across the world? The results of these have served to bring traditional

* "Understanding the New Age - World Government and World Religion" by Roy Livesey describes those groups which are significant in the movement towards world government. The United Nations is one of those groups, and significantly it is a group wherein is found much New Age influence.

19

medicine into focus.* Mrs Bailey's Theosophical Society and the U.N. are partners together, and in Geneva the WCC and the WHO are perhaps just as close. Geographically they are just 400 yards apart.

The Alice Bailey writings are prolific, and many are brought about by what is known as "automatic writing". This can be dictated by demons or they may simply guide the hand as the will is given over to them. Cases have been known of "automatic drawing" a similar occult practice giving precise replicas of old masters beautifully done and indistinguishable from the original. Alice Bailey believed that her source was a "Master"; she knew him as "The Tibetan."

Alice Bailey's books lay down the instructions for disciples in the New Age. Apart from these we can find New Age doctrine clearly expounded by Blavatsky, Teilhard de Chardin and H.G. Wells. One of Wells' least known books, "The Open Conspiracy - Blue Prints for a World Revolution" describes the New Age. In the Preface he tells us "This is my religion." I have destroyed the Alice Bailey books but among the areas noted which Mrs Bailey wrote would prepare the world for the New Age were holistic health, mind control and meditation. Music Therapy and Colour Therapy were two of the therapies mentioned.

Since 1975 the New Age movement, described in Alice Bailey's writings, has been vigorously and effectively promoting the teachings of "The Tibetan". In this way the rank and file are being brought into the New Age. The spiritual purpose of the movement is the "Invocation" of the return of "Christ" to earth. In co-operating closely with the United Nations its powerful spiritual promotion of the New World *Religion* is well anchored in a down-to-earth fashion in the machine for the promotion of the one-world government that it forsees. In fact what I believe we have is a developing situation, but do we get any indication from Scripture that the world must necessarily be turned upside down any more before Christ returns?

* For a more complete understanding see "Understanding Alternative Medicine" by Roy Livesey (3rd Edition, 1988) - New Wine Press.

I believe the answer is "no." *"While the earth remaineth, seedtime and harvest, and cold and heat, and summer and winter, and day and night shall not cease."* (Genesis 8:22).

The "Great Invocation"

The various Theosophical Society outreach groups of today promote the "Great Invocation" which is printed in dozens of languages and distributed free of charge on a vast scale. Will this thirteen-line mantra prayer be the one given to the Lord Maitreya, the Imam Mahdi, the Messiah, or whatever other name is used, when he is amongst us?

Is such a question for Christians? It is if a futurist view of prophecy is taken, and many do hold the expectation of a future Antichrist, and it is he who will be THE Christ in the eyes of the New Agers. The position I favour is that the scriptural Antichrist is fulfilled in the ongoing papacy, with the New Age serving the Roman purpose. Yet however we set the context of the New Age, and I have altered my view of this since writing the First Edition of this book, the New Age comprises much that is a danger, and as Christians, whatever our view of prophecy, we do well to be on our guard. (Proverbs 27:12).

"The Great Invocation', so innocent-sounding until we know the root and background, is at this point in time the New Age prayer to "invoke" the presence of the "Christ" on earth. This prayer certainly has had enormous promotion. For example "Readers Digest" has carried a full-page copy of "The Great Invocation".

THE GREAT INVOCATION

From the point of Light within the Mind of God
Let Light stream forth into the minds of men.
Let Light descend on Earth.

From the point of Love within the Heart of God
Let love stream forth into the hearts of men.
May Christ return to earth.

From the centre where the Will of God is known
Let purpose guide the little wills of men -
The purpose which the Masters know and serve.

From the centre which we call the race of men
Let the Plan of Love and Light work out.
And may it seal the door where evil dwells.

Let Light and Love and Power restore the Plan on Earth.

As Christians we cannot join in this prayer with the millions of others by simply substituting the name of Jesus. That is what some are inclined to do.

The "Prayer for Peace"

We cannot be unequally yoked with unbelievers. *'Be ye not unequally yoked together with unbelievers: for what fellowship hath righteousness with unrighteousness? and what communion hath light with darkness?*

And what concord hath Christ with Belial? or what part hath he that believeth with an infidel?

And what agreement hath the temple of God with idols? for ye are the temple of the living God; as God hath said, I will dwell in them, and walk in them; and I will be their God, and they shall be my people.

Wherefore come out from among them, and be ye separate, saith the Lord, and touch not the unclean thing; and I will receive you.' (2 Corinthians 6:14-17). Will "The Great Invocation" be used extensively in the body of professing-Christians? The spirit of Antichrist is at work on a broad front. Who would have believed, even five years ago, that youth in an English Anglican Church Diocese would be taught a tune for a prayer to chant in a procession of "Pilgrimage for Peace" to the Cathedral? In the Cathedral, at noon, with others chanting as they came, from other places, they were to say the "Prayer for Peace." However, and following much prayer, the "chanting" proposal was abandoned.

The same prayer, the "Prayer for Peace," reproduced from a leaflet handed out at a Roman Catholic church in Belgium a few years ago, reads as follows:

Lead me from death
to life, from falsehood to truth.
Lead me from despair
to hope, from fear to trust.
Lead me from hate
to love, from war to peace.
Let peace fill our heart,
our world, our universe.

On the back of the leaflet was written:

"Mother Teresa of Calcutta made the first public pronouncement of the prayer at an inspiring meeting in St. James's Church, Piccadilly, on 7th July 1981. The Prayer was officially launched at a significant and uplifting inter-faith service in Westminster Abbey at midday on the 6th August 1981 (Hiroshima Day).

Prayer for Peace, International Peace Centre, Kerkstraat 150, 2000 Antwerp Belgium."

St. James, Piccadilly describes itself as a New Age church. New Age is a religion but it isn't Christian.

3

New Age as a Religion

I discovered that the 1985 "Prayer for Peace" initiative, to which Mother Teresa's name was linked, was accepted by the United Nations, and the United Nations Year of Peace had begun on 24th. October. With the attacks of the enemy on so many sides it is sometimes not difficult to confuse the education of our children with evil attempts to programme them. 1984-85 was the year when many had heard of the United Nations for the first time. It was "Youth Year" at the U.N. Then followed the "Year of Peace."

The "Prayer for Peace" hand-out to the children described previously explained the "concentration of energy" when many people focus at the same time upon the same prayer. Thus, it suggested, the greatest concentration can be achieved by people saying the prayer at noon. Although the origin of the prayer was not clearly known, the multi-religious flavour of the scheme is nevertheless emphasised by the mandala, the grotesque symbolic circular figure, the religious symbol of the universe, in which the prayer was set. The effectiveness of apparently clear and simple invocations like these is that those joining in will usually do so with earnestness and zeal. They can relate to the need of the message; they miss the vague or even esoteric language in which the message is couched.

Within months of the prayer first appearing, Mother Teresa is said to have announced that its circulation was worldwide. Also according to the hand-out, the prayer was soon being said by the 900 delegates of the Assembly of World Religions convened by the Patriarch of Moscow ''to coincide with the Second United Nations Special Session on Disarmament.'' The conclusion was perhaps significant too: ''- probably the first time the world's leading religions have ever prayed together the one prayer.''

These Peace Prayers, like ''The Great Invocation'' prayer and the Hindu mantras, are an important part of the New Age. Alice Bailey was deceived but that was her message too; as to mandalas and symbols, these were to be displayed at every opportunity. Her disciples were to display New Age symbols like the all-seeing-eye of Freemasonry, the triple sixes and the rainbow.

I have been given an all-seeing-eye lapel sticker to gain entrance to a hologram exhibition in a London cathedral, and I have seen '666' formations and rainbows everywhere. Let Christians beware! God's symbol is a *real* rainbow in the sky after the rain. The New Age rainbow is a hypnotic device and New Agers call it an 'International Sign of Peace.' New Agers ''network'' together with a bond of unity between them. The rainbow is used to signal others in the network. For them it may also signify building a rainbow bridge between man and Lucifer, according to the occult tradition of the American Indians.

New Age Religion and the ''World Instant of Cooperation''

The themes of the New Age movement do not change and may be recognised by the discerning wherever New Agers are found. The focus on *protecting* the creation in the manner of the conservationists, ecologists and environmentalists, soon becomes a matter of *understanding more about* the creation, about relating to Mother Earth, being at-one with it and at-one with each other, ourselves being part of god and his creation. The key to this ''at-oneness'' is the earth's energy, the vibrations to which we are supposed to ''attune,'' as we draw our very life and strength from the earth. Yet the truth is that man lives, truly lives, *"by every word that proceedeth out of the mouth of God"* (Matthew 4:4).

New Agers despise the world and its ways, and they are angered by the Christians, usually the only ones who take the trouble to oppose their solutions. The intellectual among them, encouraged also by the demon voices in their ears, find ancient philosophies and prophecies on which to support their experience. Alas many Christians are twisting Bible verses to do the same. It is in these, not in Jesus Christ, that New Agers base their hopeless expectations of life and the future. Will the multitude of their counsels save them from the things to come any more than "the astrologers, the star gazers, the monthly prognosticators" (Isaiah 47:13) of which the bible speaks?

Especially, New Agers see the promise of a "Quantum Leap", a paradigm shift, a move into the Age of Aquarius, conscious evolution, rapid transformation, punctuated equilibrium. All of these phrases, whether from the old or the new philosophers, are New Age jargon. What is clear is that there IS a movement. The New Age movement is a very simple idea if the Christian will grasp what is involved. There are no great controversies among New Agers; they may not all know the jargon, but it is all nevertheless simple to those New Agers, vast numbers of them, who have come into what they term an "altered state of consciousness." Their world view has become completely changed. They have made their "leap." They have made their "shift." They have been transformed. Their consciousness has moved to a "higher state". In fact they have abandoned the normal human ways, including self-control. They have slipped into a passivity, inviting control by familiar spirits. They wish this for all on the planet, and they seek to bring it about.

Darwin's theory of evolution is counted by many Christians as the greatest deception of all time. Even for many who do not discern the New Age, they are clear in their belief that God most certainly did create the earth according to the Book of Genesis. Yet what we have now is a deception that is even greater, and more far reaching - not simply physical evolution, but metaphysical evolution. Not a gradual

27

evolution this time, but the conscious evolution is by a more instant shift or leap; the spiritual, supernatural, metaphysical evolution is to be a rapid "transformation."

That is what the World Instant of Cooperation (31st December 1986), the so-called "World Peace Event," was all about. The hope, based upon the energy connection of all creation, was for the Quantum Leap humanity would take when those who have already realised their divine potential would, in harmony with Mother Earth, transmit their higher consciousness all over the earth. The World Instant of Cooperation was to be the point in time when it was hoped a sufficient number, the "critical mass", would transmit this energy to all mankind, so bringing faith, love, peace and harmony throughout the world. The "Harmonic Convergence," as the name suggests, was another event with the same intention.

The "Harmonic Convergence"

In case it is thought by some that the New Age is a peculiarly American phenomenon - and the international initiatives do come from there at present - we look first at this August 16th-18th, 1987 event from a British perspective.

The leaflet available to me in the public library in Bideford in the Summer of 1987 was the first information I had seen advertising the August event. It was published in Marlborough, Wiltshire, convenient to our own occult centre, Glastonbury. As well as Glastonbury, contact addresses near various important sacred sites around the world were given. The list gives the clue to some places important to New Agers; there was Cornwall, County Donegal (Ireland), Avebury, and José Arguelles in Boulder, Colorado, who is credited with the inspiration and with the promoting of the date over twenty years. Arguelles wrote "The Mayan Factor." What is the Mayan factor, and what was the significance for the New Age of the Harmonic Convergence set for these very precise dates?

As with so much that is "New Age", the fantasy and fable can be tedious, but in this example it can be helpful to look at the detail, not only to find the root of the occult deception in this New Age event, but to evidence still further that it is not only holistic health, ouija boards, astrology, cults, Eastern religions and yoga, that are today blinding more and more. Pagan legends are being dug up to support one-off events. Just like some alternative medicines, they are presented giving little clue of the root. Christians should be able to discern the Harmonic Convergence without looking at the root of it. However some may just see folk joining together in the cause of peace and harmony. The root *is* important, and the magazine "New Frontier" (July/August 1987) puts it like this:

"From the perspective of the Mayan and Aztec calendar systems... the Mayan Quetzalcoatl, upon whose prophecies the Mayan civilisation based their calendar, August 16th 1987 marks the conclusion of a cycle of 13 heavens of 'decreasing choice,' and 9 hells of 'increasing doom.'... The last day of the hell cycles, which commenced with the landing of Cortez (in Mexico) (was) August 16th 1987. These 22 cycles are each exactly 52 years in duration. Prophecy indicates that at sunrise on the first morning of the new time (August 17th), the heart of Quetzalcoatl buried beneath the El Tule tree near Oaxaca, Mexico, will burst open, and billions of tiny spirits will emerge from the branches of the tree and implant themselves within each human heart, planting a seed of the god of peace."

Thus 17th August 1987 was seen as the dawn of the Mayan Millenium, and the date also fits Aztec prophecy. Back to the leaflet for another confirmation to the New Agers, I read a piece by Robert Coon of Glastonbury: "In the Summer of 1967, two individuals experienced prophetic visions in the Denver/Boulder, Colorado area. Both myself and Tony Shearer, a Lakota Indian, were inspired to share our vision with the public." Both visions involved the transformation of the earth in the 1980s.

That is the root of it all. What is the object of the exercise? In the leaflet, Sir George Trevelyan, the doyen of British New Agers, provides an answer: "On this date groups all over the planet gather on the sacred sites to spend two days meditating and invoking Peace and the flooding of the power of Universal Love. A phenomenon indeed, for this moment has been forseen in ancient prophecy... The cleansing change in the planet is on us, but will manifest in more violent ways if the harmonic convergence is not rightly initiated. Thus on August 16 & 17 an energy will flood through the linked network of sacred centres surrounding the globe. Earth begins to glow and become luminous. This is a time of cosmic countdown when the Light-Love-Power will flood into the suffering Earth.''

New Age Visionaries and Politicians

Leading New Age visionary, and resident of Boulder, Colorado, where the World Instant of Cooperation and the Harmonic Convergence were birthed, Barbara Marx Hubbard believes that humanity is genetically "preprogrammed" for enlightenment, and as the "New York Times Magazine" (1st May 1988) reports, her view is that a New Order is being born that will be as different from what exists now as the Renaissance was from the Middle Ages. She was the central figure behind the international New Age event, the World Instant of Cooperation on 31st December 1986.

This formidable lady was a serious contender for the Democratic Party's candidate as Vice-President of the United States in 1984. At a Roman Catholic church in Boulder she said that with twenty of her friends they "visualised" her becoming the nominee. It happened! I saw on video her address to the Democratic Party following the campaign. Apart from what we may discern from the speech, this arrival of "New Age Power" in "Power Politics" makes the event of special interest. Yet we were also to witness in 1988 the possibility of a Kingdom/Dominion/Christian Reconstruction President. That was Pat Robertson, and his "Secret Kingdom"* can be regarded as the "Christian" counterpart of Hubbard's ideas for world cooperation.

* published by Bantam Books, New York, 1982. This sets out the "Eight Laws of the Secret Kingdom" and we return to the teaching of this book in chapter seven.

I transcribed the final part of Barbara Marx Hubbard's address following her campaign for the nomination as Vice-President to Walter Mondale. She spoke of the rainbow. In the Harmonic Convergence (1987) there is the expectation of a new tribe, "the Warriors of the Rainbow" in line with ancient American Indian belief, to restore the earth to its former beauty. Then in Winchester Cathedral in England in the same year the "Rainbow Covenant" was launched - a covenant "between us and God, us and our neighbour, and us and nature."

Barbara Marx Hubbard, in 1984, had spoken of the "Rainbow Coalition." The text of her speech which follows offers another valuable opportunity to discern the New Age position of one who is both a prominent New Ager and a politician.

"... The Rainbow Coalition is bringing together all colours and races. It is also now the coalescing of the mind with the heart. It is now time for a new marriage. We should have a wedding in the White House. It is the wedding of love and knowledge, of spirit and material power. Our forbears set forth a vision. It is written on the dollar bill as it is written in our hearts - E Pluribus Unum - "out of many one". "Novus Ordo Seclorum" - a new order of the ages. You see the unfinished pyramid of the cosmic eye. This means that when we combine our magnificent building power with our spirit and love we will have *a new order of the ages*. And finally it says, "Annuit Coeptis" - God favours this enterprise. This means that we are not doing this work alone. The Force is with us. It is the intention of creation that human beings cooperate to build a world in which all people are free to do their best. It is to this new order that we must now recommit. It's the tradition of America. It's transformation. We must go forth from this place with a vision of the future equal to our capacity. We have the first woman Vice President, Geraldine Ferraro, to bring feminine power to nurture the potential of the world. I support her totally and enthusiastically. The family of America joined with the family of the world from whence we come is the new coalition. Together we shall go to the mountain top. In this

31

campaign, Martin, Robert, Malcolm and John, Socrates and Jesus, Galileo and Ghandi, we pledge to you who have climbed this mountain before us alone, that this time we are coming together. They can kill us one by one, but they can never kill us if we join hands and climb together. Through you we have caught a glimpse of the human race acting at its highest. Now the united party and people, we can act out the dream. What can I contribute to this magnificent effort? With your help I can gather the people to build... the future in this administration. I have spent the last twenty-years discovering the new ideas at work. My credentials are in the future. I too am the daugther of an American immigrant who came to the city of Hope, New York City. In 1776 a handful of genius came together to take the first step. In 1984 it will not be a *hand*ful, it will be a *land* full of genius. We will gather in every town, in every village, in every city in new town meetings of the future to envision the possible society, to seek common goals, to match our needs with our resources, and to cooperate to create the world we choose. We will think globally, and act locally. This must be a campaign for a positive future. I propose that we do not spend a single penny or waste a single moment of time on that which divides us, because a house divided against itself cannot stand. It is time to unite, not just Democrats with Democrats, but all Americans in a common cause. The cause of America is the cause of the world. Let the Democrats go forth not only as a united force, but as a *uniting* force for this nation, and we shall work together to fulfil the dream. We will state the word of truth from the place of power in the American presidency. When the word of our potential goes forth from the American presidency, the word shall be made flesh. In 1776 they alligned to do it. They committed to it, and they co-created it. So must we, and so shall it be. I thank you very much for this opportunity. I look forward to supporting Walter Mondale and Geraldine Ferraro in our quest for the presidency. Thank you.'' (applause).

Remarkable though that text may appear, especially perhaps to British readers, we may well reflect upon how nearly Barbara Marx Hubbard became Vice-President, and if Mondale had beaten Reagan, the Republican! Politics in the U.S. is very different from Britain. It might have been a very near thing. Occult visualisation is powerful. But Hubbard, mother and grandmother, was not finished! Visualisation or visions, it's all the same if you're a New Ager.

Another of Barbara's visions is one of global unity active in "citizen diplomacy" with the Soviet Union. The "New York Times Magazine"* article includes this startling report: "New Agers imbued with a vision of global unity have been especially active in citizen diplomacy with the Soviet Union. Barbara, among others, enlisted 100 Russian representatives for a "Soviet-American Citizens' Summit" last February in Washington. The Russian delegates attended a joint meditation under the auspices of the Pentagon Meditation Club, a group of 15 Department of Defence employees who, through meditation, hope to place a "spiritual aura" of peace around the planet."

Barbara Marx Hubbard was the driving force behind the World Instant of Cooperation. This was an event with supposedly multi-millions of participants. Her views are in line with those given by John Randolph Price's Spirit Guide, "Asher" through whose instructions the W.I.C. event seems to have been planned. Along similar lines to Asher, Barbara writes of the cleansing of a destructive element in the population**:

"One fourth is destructive. They are born angry with God. They hate themselves. They project this hatred on to the world. They are defective seeds.

There have always been defective seeds. In the past they were permitted to die a 'natural death'. Their bodies were recycled to new life and their souls reincarnated in bodies capable of receiving signals from the higher self.

The 'evil' personality is one who suffers the defects of a disconnection between the higher self and the ego. The higher

---

* "Colorado's Thriving Cults" by Fergus M. Bordewich (1st May 1988) Copyright © 1988 by The New York Times Company. Reprinted by Permission.
** "The Book of Co-Creation - An evolutionary Interpretation of the New Testament, Part III (The Revelation Alternatives to Armageddon)."

self cannot get through. The silver cord is severed.

We have no choice dearly beloveds. It is a case of the destruction of the whole planet or the elimination of the ego-driven godless one fourth who at this time of planetary birth can't be allowed to live on to reproduce their defective disconnection and destroy forever the opportunity of Homo Sapiens to become Homo Universalis heirs of God.

Before this stage of power can be inherited by the God-centered members of the social body-the self-centered members must be destroyed. There is no alternative. Only the God-centered can evolve. Only the good endures.

Fortunately you dearly beloveds are not responsible for this act. We are. We are in charge of God's selection process for planet Earth. He selects. We destroy. We are the riders of the pale horse death to those who are unable to know God. We do this for the sake of the World. Now everything is global and connected. Each person is about to inherit the power of destruction and co-creation. At this level of individual Christ-like power which you are to inherit as the sons and daughters of God everyone must personally know God's design."

In another place in the book Barbara Marx Hubbard writes: "All those souls who are less energetic will not pass on in new bodies. They will either play out their education elsewhere, or choose extinction. They will not be allowed to reincarnate on planet earth.

"Once the tribulations are over, and the devil of separation is destroyed forever, no more self-centred humans will incarnate on earth. This type of human personality will be quickly extincted, never to rise again. Like Neanderthal, like the dinosaur, they are gone forever.

"The souls-in-waiting are impatient for the day of judgment. They wish to be incarnated as living sons of God..."

The Bible is forthright with many direct and challenging statements which would present a horror picture to many, were they able to register what is written there. I would not wish to draw too close an analogy to the way, as Christians, we can view New Age writings, but it would not be right

34

to suppose that they come from uncaring people, neglectful of their neighbours or who are insincere. Such is rarely the case. We are not to be alarmed by their words and we do well to note what these leaders say, and for our understanding of the New Age we pull out the essential doctrines of energies, higher consciousness, etc, looking at the way different New Agers apply these concepts. We do that to aid our own understanding, but we go further as we alert to the awakening of New Age on the political agenda. The United Nations views the population problem in a similar way, and in "Understanding the New Age - World Government and World Religion," I describe the relevance of a secret group, the Club of Rome, to the planning of population. The 766-page "Global 2000 Report to President Carter" tells us on its first page, "our conclusions are disturbing." Can we be surprised if New Age ideas, reflecting the large New Age voter list in countries like America and eventually Britain, find outlet in New Age politicians?

The "World Instant of Cooperation" (W.I.C) and the Spirit Guide "Asher"

If Barbara Marx Hubbard was the driving force behind the W.I.C., the whole event seems to have been planned on the instructions of the demon "Asher" speaking to John Randolph Price and quoted in his book "Practical Spirituality."* Price is the founder of The Quartus Foundation which has the objective to "continually document the truth that man is a spiritual being possessing all the powers of the spiritual realm... that man is indeed God individualised; and that as man realises his true identity, he becomes a Master Mind with dominion over the material world."

According to the information sheet on the W.I.C. sent out from Boulder: at Noon Greenwich time, and at 5 a.m. Mountain time on 31st December 1986 "50,000,000 people

* published by Quartus Books, P.O. Box 1768, Boerne, TX 78006, USA - 1985 John R. Price is the initiator of the annual global prayer for world peace every 31st December.

from around the world will be asked to suspend, for one hour, all thoughts of fear, conflict and separation as they pray, meditate and contemplate the oneness of all life on earth. Another 500,000,000 will be asked to endorse this time of harmonious resonance. A sufficient mass of people focusing for a sufficient period of time on an image of global peace and harmony can help change the consciousness of our planet for the benefit of all living things.''

The average reader of that information sheet is not troubled by any of it. He may dismiss it as barmy! He may give it a try! Or he may be fully taken in by it! Certainly few are bothered by it. Neither are we as Christians to be troubled by any of this, nor by the sinister picture that emerges as we look carefully at what New Age leaders like Barbara Marx Hubbard and John Randolph Price believe.

Rather we are to be clear from Scripture by the Spirit of God that what they speak of spiritual things is deception. We are not to give audience to words spoken by demons. A danger in looking at the New Age is that we may give credibility even to any small detail of what demons, through Hubbard, Price or anyone else, would put before us. Yet with the truth of God's Word clear to us, we are able to be watchful, even warning of the deceptions as they appear. The devil will use one tactic after another moving in the areas where he finds us vulnerable. We are not to fear, nor heed, the doctrines of devils. God says, *"My son, give me thine heart, and let thine eyes observe my ways"* (Proverbs 23: 26). With the rise of figures like Hubbard on the political scene at a high level, and given the temptation to many Christians to participate in politics under the banner of "Christian Reconstruction", christianising the world instead of evangelising the lost, it does seem right to analyse the hidden and not-so-hidden agenda of these politicians.

Price's "Practical Spirituality", containing the hidden agenda for the W.I.C., is dated 1985. On page 18 he relates the message received from Asher as to the "fusing of energies which will reach a peak on 31st December 1986." Reporting the message, Price writes of the removal of the threat of global war, dramatic advances in scientific

36

discoveries, a revamped concept of religion and church. This "fusing of energies" would serve as a ring of protection for "more than 3 billion people." Here we see a separation among the human race; what of the remainder, more than 2½ billion people? The answer is that Asher's number "represents those already on the spiritual path..." Price heard the demon put it this way, and I quote:

"Nature will soon enter her cleansing cycle. Those who reject the earth changes with an attitude of 'it can't happen here' will experience the greatest emotion of fear and panic, followed by rage and violent action. These individuals, with their lower vibratory rates, will be removed during the next two decades. Those who expect change and face it calmly with faith will move through it virtually untouched and will be the builders of the future." This message was at the root of the W.I.C., the World Healing/Peace Meditation. In New Age terms it truly was big - and successful. The figures look on the high side to me; however "varying estimates indicate that... (the W.I.C) involved 100,000,000 - 500,000,000 persons meeting in thousands of locations around the world..."* On any view it is a serious situation.

* "America: The Sorcerer's New Apprentice - The Rise of New Age Shamanism" by Dave Hunt and T.A. McMahon (Harvest House, U.S.A., 1988).

4

New Age Centres and Leaders

Findhorn: Anchoring the New Age in "Planet Earth"

No book about the New Age can ever be complete; no definition of the New Age can ever be complete. Certainly no book can be completed, nor any definition acceptable without a reference to the goings-on at Findhorn in Scotland! The community there in its early days was famous for the cabbages which were known to grow to even more than 40 lbs in weight. In a barren sand delphiniums grew to 8 feet and roses bloomed in the snow. At Findhorn we find the counterfeit of much to be indentified in the Christian life. As time has moved on, and the level of spiritual awareness increased, there came about a reduced desire there for the "signs and wonders." As Christians it becomes that way too. We are to keep our focus off signs (Matthew 12:39) and put it on Jesus Christ. Satan, (or Pan, the Devas, and the elves and elementals, as those at Findhorn would prefer to call them) has moved Findhorn on in the New Age scheme of things.

The New Age view is of a Britain dotted with "power points" connected together with "ley lines". This is an area with which I am familiar from my own experience, having dowsed with a pendulum, and located these lines and points in various exercises when a full-time "searcher" in the occult realm. These ley lines were said to be energy channels which gave off an energy power, often known as "good vibrations", where undisturbed. The power was particularly good where the lines joined or crossed. However where the lines are disturbed, perhaps by earth workings or road building, the energy flow is said to be adverse. Suffice to say here, the Findhorn community was established where a "power point" was located.

As the founder of the Findhorn community would say, it was no accident that he went there. Yet of course there is no basis in science for the idea of the ley lines, the "power points", the spirit beings, nor yet for the cabbages that grew sometimes beyond 40 lbs in weight. Why then 40 lb cabbages? The Bible tells us that Satan can masquerade as an angel of light and at Findhorn he got the attention of a few people! I don't know what was the norm for a cabbage in the Garden of Eden but despite the fertilisation of crops, it seems likely in these days that the ecologists are right when they say that hardly any part of our world can escape pollution of one sort or another. The evil by-products of Satan's rulership are surely very numerous in terms of their effect on the creation. It is within Satan's power to heal the earth in this limited way, just as we know of counterfeit healing of mortal bodies. This leaves a greater price in terms of body, soul or spirit to be paid. In the same way those cabbages have been a mighty advertisement for Satan's ways.

How then is the Findhorn garden viewed in retrospect by those involved there? In "The Magic of Findhorn" we can read the view of the head gardener that the growth was extraordinary to demonstrate that it was possible. He tells us:

Now we know it is possible to work with the Nature Kingdom, but we no longer have the need to produce a plant where it won't normally grow. Just because some of these plants were growing in the middle of the cold and dry sand it didn't mean they were happy about it. They were there to show the power and potential of co-operation. *

The philosophy of Findhorn, like that of the Hindu, is that Man can be "at one" with the creation, with the spirit world and - it follows - with God himself. "Findhorn was an experiment in the co-operation among three kingdoms" Paul Hawken tells us. They were Man, the Devas and the Nature Spirits. The Devas are the Hindu gods of the celestial powers. "A Guide to the Gods"*, a compendium of the names of

* "The Magic of Findhorn" by Paul Hawken (published by Souvenir Press Ltd - London).

* Compiled by Richard Clayton (Heinemann/Quixote - 1981).

some 1,400 deities, tells us their name derives from "dyaus", the bright sky, from which they were supposed to have come, and the opposite of the "asuras" who were the demons. We find that throughout the world of the occult there is some awareness of "evil spirits" apart from the good. What is not realised is the truth that Satan masquerades as an angel of light and that the manifestations they see, whether through elves, pixies or the extraordinary things that are produced, *all* result from the work of demons.

Yet I believe Findhorn is something more than just another centre for turning out New Agers and introducing its visitors to the supernatural powers found there. Christian ministers can often, it seems, become frustrated when they find that what they teach, and what their flocks say they believe, does not match up with what is found in the lives they lead. Findhorn was already the New Age *in practice* when its founder, Peter Caddy, attended a New Age conference in 1965 called by Sir George Trevelyan. Peter Caddy told them:

We are practising what is being talked about. We are building a New Age community at Findhorn right now. We are not talking about it. You can't make a charter for the New Age. There are no blueprints. We have been told by God through Eileen (his wife) that we are to live in the moment, guided by God. It is His plan, not ours. Let it be revealed through Him. Patterns are revealed when looking back, not when looking ahead. **

Lacking discernment many pastors might not quarrel with that statement. As to the commitment evidenced there, and as to the faith, many long to see that among Christians. Need we doubt that Satan is working earnestly and effectively in his counterfeit way?

Satan seeks to counterfeit all that is of God. He does it with the occult power at his disposal using men and women who take their eyes off God, only found in the Lord Jesus Christ. He builds *men* with his occult counterfeits. He builds *a society* including through the network of the New Age movement. Findhorn is a very important part of that network. It is showing the world that the New Age works *in practice*.

** "The Magic of Findhorn".

In New Age language, it is anchoring the spiritual realm into the world itself.

One New Age: Different Perspectives

The New Age movement is vast and encompasses a great many groups. It will not be surprising to see a different perspective coming from each according to its place in the movement and the overall plan.

A Christian girl who was once a member of the Findhorn community, reflects this in *her* perspective of what is the New Age. She writes:

In the New Age there is a marked emphasis on Nature. The beliefs are pantheistic, seeing divinity within everything, but this is attuned to by meditation, rather than worshipped as an idol. Even man-made objects are treated as personalities - cars and machines are given names, and the labels on the drawers for kitchen utensils in Findhorn say "Metal beings" and "Wooden beings".

As she understood the New Age it was to be an age of service, of living in harmony, or attunement with the planet and with each other. It would be an age of groups and communities, people living, working and learning together where the whole is seen to be greater than the sum of its parts. This concept, called "synergy", is the strength of the movement. What we see is a powerful network of groups, all ready for the New Age. At Findhorn they focus on the creation and find devas (gods) and lower beings (the elementals) at work in amongst the gardens with the 40 lb cabbages.

New Age Philosophers

Following New Age philosophers like Alice Bailey, H.G. Wells and Teilhard de Chardin, there came onto the scene a new and younger personality, David Spangler. It was no mere coincidence that he went to Findhorn, stayed there for a good length of time, and added greatly to the development of the community. In David Spangler there was found the philosophy to match the practice. He feels Findhorn is the first community to 'solidly ground the energies of an entirely new type, not from new sources, but of a new vibration.'*

In witchcraft, the occult and the New Age much is esoteric. In other words the language is only clear to the initiated. Progress is difficult to make until all of the hidden meaning is understood. For example in Freemasonry initiation is through a number of degrees from one to thirty-three. It is a *process* and the deceived are gently taken further, exposed further and trusted further. Eventually the mind can be fully captured with the realisation that the purpose is full-blown worship of Lucifer (or Satan). Initiation is involved in every area of the occult. One step leads to another, and it is the same in the New Age movement. David Spangler is a leader in the movement.

He has moved on since his years at Findhorn. He has given at least one sermon in the prestigious Episcopal Cathedral of St. John the Divine, in Manhattan - a eucharistic sermon at that! He helped develop the vision of the Baca Grande in Colorado.

The Baca Grande in Colorado

In March 1988 the Lord made the way for my visit to Colorado U.S.A., a state of much New Age activity. I was able to visit various New Age centres including in Baca Grande in the San Luis Valley.

The idea for the visit to America was first sparked by an article in "The Valley Courier" a newspaper sent from the San Luis Valley. I read of a couple who had moved to the area and who "are conjunctively the stimulus behind the plans which are gradually turning the area into a microcosm of the world's different religions and cultures." The couple are Mr and Mrs Maurice Strong, and in Mrs Hanne Strong's words to the interviewer: "It could only happen with the combination of him and I... I have the vision and he is the manifester." This could have been but an ordinary story but the newspaper carried a photograph which got my attention. It showed Mrs Strong, her adopted father Red Indian Chief Robert Smallboy and Pope John-Paul II meeting at the Vatican in 1982.

* "The Magic of Findhorn".

43

I read that Mrs Strong's eight year old grandson born in the San Luis Valley went by a different name when travelling in Tibet where he is known as Rechung Tulku - the reincarnation of an 11th Century Tibetan saint named Rechung Dorje Drakpa. Mrs Strong told of the signs while being driven home from hospital with the baby, signs that the baby's upbringing would not be consistent with that of most children in the San Luis Valley. The newspaper quotes Mrs Strong who saw 'these incredible black spots in the sky.'' They were eagles. ''They were flying in formation - 32 golden and bald eagles flying together, which they never do. So I knew it was a sign that he was a holy child.'' Two years later in 1981 a high Lama from Tibet recognised him as being the reincarnation of the 11th Century saint and a formal announcement with a ''letter of Discovery'' soon followed. Apparently high Lamas traditionally leave notes saying where and under what conditions they will be reborn and Rechung Dorje Drakpa had written that he would be reborn on the American continent, in the largest alpine valley in the world.

That valley is the San Luis Valley, and when he was four the boy was formally enthroned in Tibet. My own destination was the San Luis Valley. I was surrounded by beautiful wilderness.

To drive me there God had given me a new friend who told me about the recent World Wilderness Congress and the plan for the World Conservation Bank. One significant participant at the Congress, along with David Rockefeller and Edmond de Rothschild, had been Maurice Strong, perhaps the leading environmentalist figure at the United Nations, and the owner of the Baca Grande.

Describing Maurice Strong's accomplishments in regard to the important United Nations Stockholm Conference which was the first to identify ecological concerns, the ''Rocky Mountain Magazine'' reported: The 1972 conference was the first ever to assemble leaders of international and developing nations to confront global issues such as acid rain, pollution, and deforestation, and to set up specific international programmes to deal with them. Strong ran the show and, against considerable odds, made it an unqualified success.

As regards the Baca, as Mrs Strong has said, she has the vision for the Baca Grande in the San Luis Valley; Mr Strong is the "manifester". I visited New Age centres among the many that are springing up. It is a place where big New Age "names" gather. In Mrs Strong's own words to "Baca Grande News": "The Baca can be a teaching centre on a grand scale."

At the Baca there is a vision of World Harmony. I found kind and caring people, sincere people whom we are to witness to. Yet the Bible doesn't speak of World Harmony. It tells of deception for the world. It tells of a deceived heart for the sinner who turns aside after attractive but fake religious systems *"that he cannot deliver his soul, nor say, Is there not a lie in my right hand?"* (Isaiah 44:20).

The Vision for the Baca Grande

We are not mainly concerned here with "the world" and with humanism. We look at counterfeit spirituality and at the concept of the global village at the Baca Grande. What is the background? "The Valley Courier," the newspaper of the San Luis Valley, gives the answer: It was around Christmas 1978 when the prophet came down from the mountains... He was an old man, regarded widely as a mystic... He walked to the house of Maurice and Hanne Strong who had just moved to the area... Mrs Strong said, "The first thing he said was 'I've been waiting for you to arrive.'" According to Mrs Strong, "He spent the next four days with us, and he told us what was going to happen here. He also told me that I would have to do it." The "it" referred to would soon come to occupy the daily energies of Mrs Strong. It would also come to attract the attention and, in many cases, suspicion of onlookers throughout the country and world. "He said people would come from all over the world to learn here."

The man had apparently evisioned the global village many years back. According to Mrs Strong, one story tells of a day, "fifteen to twenty years ago," when he was found standing on the land where a restaurant called the Bistro now

45

stands, "crying like a baby." "He was standing there, saying, 'Where's the village?'" she says. "He had already seen it." Mrs Strong adds that, "In his prophecies, he said it would be a foreigner who would do it." Strong is Canadian; Mrs Strong was born and raised in Denmark.

The vision started to assume physical shape in early 1979 when Strong contracted to grant land for a Tibetan monastery and village. Then within three months there was a grant for Lindisfarne, an association of individuals and groups around the world dedicated to fostering the emergence of a new global structure. The headquarters of the Lindisfarne Assocation is located in the Cathedral of St. John the Divine in Manhattan, a church well known for its New Age activity. The Very Rev. James Parks Morton, Dean of the Cathedral is a member of the Lindisfarne board. Now in place, and the centre of things at the Baca, is the chapel following a dome shaped style of sacred architecture. A small community exists and is dedicated to the discovery of "the traditions of sacred cosmology in the arts and crafts, with particular focus on the study and construction of sacred architecture."

Next at the Baca Grande came a grant for the Aspen Institute for Humanistic Studies. Strong, himself a trustee of Aspen, offered 300 acres and it was accepted. The Institute built both a seminar centre and housing for visiting dignatories, in what promised to be a more secluded and appropriate atmosphere than the Ritzy Colorado tourist city of Aspen when it came to humanistic education. I read that Henry Kissinger visited and that Jim Callaghan attended one of the Institute's seminars.

For Mrs Strong it was the arrival of native Indians who were of particular interest. Shamans used to come to various power points along the mountains in search of knowledge. "Holy people," Mrs Strong says "would come here to fast and pray for their own spiritual empowerment." Now a group of Indian elders from all over the continent came after she had been told of the old man's vision. They said the old man was right. The Indians' own vision aligned with that of the old man who claimed to be the reincarnation of the Sioux Chief Gall. The vision was interpreted like this:

"... that when mankind's spiritual base becomes so weakened as to be near collapse, the world's different religious groups, will gather on the land around (the Baca) where 'the preparation for the new world will take place.' So basically, they are saying the new age will develop here, using the background of all the great religions of the world. They'll work to recognise the common source - the origin of all the religions - and they'll use that to build the new age."

There we have the false prophecy; there we have the New Age vision. Other New Agers have visions that are different, yet they all have much in common. The Christian sees the unity of the many who will take the broad way that leads to destruction. We have seen how the Baca vision came about; now let us see what has resulted, what I found when I visited the Baca Grande.

Discovering the Baca Grande

The Baca stretches over 100,000 acres of prime rangeland. It is the last surviving parcel of five land grants awarded to the Spanish Maria Baca family. Armed with a map showing a lot of open space, with difficulty, we set off to discover the various developments. I was helped by various news cuttings. For example I had already read "The Valley Courier" (21 April 1987). It carried a photograph of Hanne Strong with the caption that described the dropping of "a banana into the flames" with Sheila Devi "who sings most of the ceremony in Sanskrit." This was described as "part of an ancient ceremony practised each day behind the Aspen Institute for Humanistic Studies."

I read, also in "The Valley Courier", of 200 acres of land donated to His Holiness the 16th Gyalwa Karmapa, head of the Kagyu Order of Tibetan Buddhism and that "His Holiness" had developed a vision of a community of Tibetans at the Baca; it was anticipated that 100 monks and lay-people from India, Nepal and Bhutan would be relocated there.

These Tibetan monks were not yet established but one of the first communities I discovered was known as the Zen Centre. Here we were welcomed by one of the many caring people to be found in the New Age movement, a young woman. There were at that time few in residence and there was the opportunity to be shown around this Buddhist centre. The teacher there was Zenatsu Richard Baker-roshi, and, to our surprise, our guide added, "Richard Baker teaches Rockefeller." In his story of Sangha, a Zen Practice Community, Baker-roshi tells us that Zen means concentration or absorption in which you are one with everything. He tells us that the dominant bonding and controlling aspect of the Zen Centre community is meditation together and the sharing of a daily schedule.

Rome among the Religions at the Baca

We learned there were sports fixtures between the Zen Centre and the Carmelites. From there we went to the Carmelite Nada community. Again I have the advantage of readable articles from the local press, and in the course of a several-page story (September 1987) "The High Valley Independent" tells us: Nada means 'nothing.'

More formally they are known as the Roman Catholic Carmelite Order of the Spiritual Life Institute, and their spiritual founder is said to be Elijah the prophet. All numbers are small, and perhaps there is a thousand acres per person at the Baca, and in 1987 there were just nine Carmelites, with six more in Nova Scotia, Canada. Numbers were small yet there was a sense that here was something important in the New Age scheme. Here at the Nada Hermitage they support the new chapel and publish a well presented magazine, "Desert Call." I bought the latest edition and was able to read that this little Spiritual Life Institute had been founded "with a mandate from the visionary Pope John XXIII" in 1960. That was when the present wave of Roman Catholic ecumenism really began, and here at the Baca was an *"ecumenical* monastic community of men and women who embrace a vowed life of contemplative servitude."

As will no doubt be clearer in later chapters, there is much in the New Age which, because of its spirituality, makes no sense to the natural mind. Here at the Nada I had found a community that was both Roman Catholic and New Age. The following, describes a "Cassette Retreat" on "Christian

Humanism'' by William McNamara, the founder: Laying the foundations for prayer in a rich, vibrant, natural life, Fr. William deplores the narcissism, fanaticism and utilitarianism that obstruct full human vitality and tells us how to become 'disciplined wild men.' He describes the Internal Trinity in each of us... advocates praying the Our Father backwards, and gives remarkably practical advice on spiritual reading, meditation.

Thus it can be said the Carmelites at the Baca are not the run of the mill Roman Catholic group! We need not be surprised to read (Rocky Mountain News, 25 October 1987) that there has been some crossing over between communities, with the Carmelites being the most active ambassadors between the new religious groups and the residents.

I found nearly everything at the Baca to be New Age, if not so obviously religious. At the foot of the beautiful Sangre de Cristo mountains can be found the World Unity Garden growing plants representing today's major food crops. Central in New Age philosophy is the idea of a universal force or energy, which has no basis in science. We meet it in the Unity Garden where we find a large crystal which, according to the Director, ''emanates light and radiates energy from the centre of the earth enhancing the growth patterns of the plants and helping them grow in harmony.'' The ''Valley Courier'' (12 October 1987) reported a ''Symbolised Seed Exchange'' at the Garden. The ceremony was again one performed by Mrs Strong and it included ''smudging'' the seeds. Smudging, the sacred ritual of purifying with smoke, comes from the Indian native people of America. Auroville, a city of Global Unity in India which derived its inspiration from Sri Aurobindo's vision of the future evolution of man, was represented at the exchange.

The development of man irrespective of religion and nationality is the main consideration according to the founder of the Sri Aurobindo Centre now established at the Baca. The ideal is to seek a quality of life and nurture an environment, which are ''intimately related to each other and to the ideal of individual and social perfection.''

Another philosophy! Yet the essential feature of New Age

groups sooner or later becomes the search for a "new consciousness" (or "higher consciousness"). There are many ways of attaining this. The Tibetans will have already attained it back in Tibet! Baker-roshi is teaching it at the Zen Centre. The Carmelites are achieving it through their silence and strange meditations. At the Sri Aurobindo learning centre, the seminars, workshops and courses are simply variations on the same theme, little or no different from the ways I myself employed, both as an individual and in various groups when I was a searcher and New Ager. The end result is the same whatever religious label is attached. Sooner or later man discovers that he is a 'god' and is in control.

Of course man is mistaken. He is deceived. It is the same lie of the serpent to Eve in the Garden of Eden. She was invited to eat the fruit of the Tree of Knowledge, and the serpent told her the lie that she whould be as god: *"Ye shall not surely die: For God doth know that in the day ye eat thereof, then your eyes shall be opened, and ye shall be as gods, knowing good and evil"* (Genesis 3:4-5). She believed the lie. She was disobedient. Eve looked elsewhere and not to God.

All within a period of a few months before my visit, yet another press report ("High Valley Independent" - August 1987) tells of the "Ground-breaking ceremony at the Haidakhandi Universal Ashram at the Baca. The significance is Earth Worship, and worship is also offered to the mineral kingdom, the animal kingdom and the plant kingdom. Before the temple can be built, the beings that live in the underworld also have to be offered prayers. Prayers are offered to the "protectors of the eight directions" and all the planets of the zodiac, and there had to be invocation to Lord Gauesha, seen as the master of all created things. The news report showed a scale model of what looked like a very fine temple building - to be erected to the Divine Universal Mother.

Of course readers may counter: don't we see pagan and religious temples springing up all over Britain? What is so special about a remote high valley beneath the Rocky Mountains? The difference is that here in the Baca we have ecumenical communities. Just what will be the eventual significance of a "mandate from Pope John XXIII" for the ecumenical Carmelite Spiritual Life Institute, we shall have to see. But there is much indication that the Rome of Revelation 17, and the papal dynasty seen by the great men of God through the ages as "that antichrist" of 1 John 2:18, is embarked upon wooing the pagan religions, the earth worshippers and the New Agers into the world church. The very name "Temple to the Divine Universal Mother" suggests common ground that the Mother harlot of Rome can move in on. Will not "hand join in hand" in the name of the unity and peace to which all these groups subscribe? (Proverbs 11:21).

"We wrestle not against flesh and blood, but against principalities, against powers, against the rulers of the darkness of this world, against spiritual wickedness in high places" (Ephesians 6:12). Accordingly, it would be wrong to make much of the main personalities in the Baca, and after all, Mrs Strong is the wife of the grantor of the land, a natural choice for ceremonies in any society.

Another ceremony attended by Mrs Strong was "to Antanta, the king of snakes... to appease Mother Earth... a gesture of gratitude for all the grace that the earth gives to humankind... to appease the nine planets..." Ceremonies like these are described in 2 Kings 23:5 but they are such that the average news reporter would not readily comprehend. It makes no sense to him! Yet it makes a good story! But Christians at least need to wake up! These are deluded people but they are not cranks. They are not crazy. Although it is counterfeit, it is spiritual reality. Also reporting *can* be well informed. The ceremonies were *presided* over by a "qualified" priestess, who was able to write the report with some understanding.

Environmentalism is an entry point to the New Age, and there is no shortage of occult and New Age within the ranks of the United Nations. Maurice Strong has been the UN's Environmental specialist for nearly two decades, yet it would be wrong to suggest that Strong neccessarily has any real understanding of spiritual life at the Baca. To make a human conspiracy theory out of all the connections would not be

51

right. To make connections and coincidences would be to fall into the same trap as the New Ager. He marvels at the global community growing up at the Baca, and he reckons the spirits are on his side.

Priestess or Performer?
Entrepreneur or Altruist?

I don't see conspiracy at the Baca. I do see the Baca Grande as a training ground, where the world may learn about world religion and world government. It is an important New Age workshop.

The impression I am left with is that Mr and Mrs Maurice Strong are a hard-working, well-meaning, extraordinarily influential couple, and patrons for the land in that beautiful valley. As in the earth-breaking ceremony, Hanne is surely a performer and not the actual priestess. But for her standing and position, isn't she the average New Ager, perhaps still a searcher and waiting to be reached with the Gospel of Jesus Christ? (Proverbs 25:25).

With Maurice Strong, the question is a different one. In the words of "Canadian Business" (April 1983), it is: entrepreneur or altruist? We read, "Canadian business leaders have never known quite what to make of Strong... The details of his biography read like a mixture of Jack London, Dag Hammarskjold and Armand Hammer... He operates at a level of international awareness shared by only a few Canadians (Pierre Trudeau is one of them)." He protects the creation while Hanne seems set to discover more about the secrets of the creation, but, as the magazine notes, "there is a spiritual dimension to Strong's world view... Strong is deeply attracted to the insights of Buddhism and says he has more than once considered dropping out to pursue a life of contemplation. He and Hanne both meditate and practise yoga and are followers of the Karma Pa, a Tibetan religious leader who has more Tibetan devotees than does the Dalai Lama."

That is how "Canadian Business" described Mr and Mrs Strong's religious leanings. However it is right to make it clear that, while it is true that the couple do meditate, and

52

whilst they had a very high regard for the Karma-Pa, they do not count themselves his followers in the sense of having become Buddhists.

However there seems little doubt that Maurice Strong cares about the environment and understands the problems. In the words of a Christian friend involved with environmental questions at a high level, and who has talked with Strong in different parts of the world, ''those who clamour against ecological destruction are not making it all up.'' He was present at the Governing Council meeting for the United Nations Environment Programme in Nairobi in 1974 when Strong, the programme's Executive Director, presented his Report. ''That conference,'' my Christian friend tells me, ''woke me up to the terrible state of the world environment.'' And he adds that Strong ''does know about the environmental breakdown and has the financial wherewithall to help in some way.''

Since 1966 when the Prime Minister of Canada asked Strong to run Canada's external aid programme, Strong has channelled his entrepreneurial energies into a world-wide network of foreign-aid projects, and in the words of ''Canadian Business'', ''built a global network of contacts among top people in the Third World, which led to his selection as the key organiser of the 1972 U.N. Conference on the Human Environment in Stockholm. It was a masterful feat of diplomacy; Strong managed to get the representatives of 112 nations to agree unanimously to a global plan for environmentally sound world development.'' In 1970 he had been appointed as the U.N's Under Secretary General, with special responsibility for the environment. Here was a man with authority given by the rulers of nations. Here we find men with big jobs to do, and for whom we are to pray (1 Timothy 2:1-2).

We don't write to condemn any of the leaders at the Baca Grande or of the New Age; it is the *story* that is important here. Yet people are the most important, and nearer to God's heart than any scheme or plan. As Christians we are not able to change the world from the way God has ordained it according to Scripture. We are not to try to christianise the world. We are not called to complain, as some Christians are doing, at the efforts the world is making. Our Lord did not complain of Caesar. He said, *"... Render therefore unto Caesar the things which be Caesar's, and unto God the things which be God's"* (Luke 20:25). We are to evangelise souls - and that includes New Agers too, whatever their walk in life.

We have to look further at this New Age movement in the following pages, but as we do so, let us not forget the personal need of those locked in there. As Christians we have found new life in Jesus Christ. New Agers have found a spiritual counterfeit, and yet they receive the Gospel through you or through me. *"He that winneth souls is wise"* (Proverbs 11:30) and true believers are the light in a dark and deceived world (Matthew 5:14-16).

Visit to Sedona - Energy Centre in Arizona!

From Colorado I came to Arizona to meet with a researcher who provided information for the oustandingly successful American Christian books exposing the New Age. It was early April 1988, with the temperature 100 degrees in Phoenix where I was met for the drive north to the cooler mountain region and the town of Sedona. My immediate impression on arriving was that this must be one of the most beautiful and climatically perfect places on the face of the earth.

The bright red rocks and canyons looked truly magnificent. I couldn't help thinking that if one ever was thinking of "dropping out" there could be no better place in which to do it. Many do go to Sedona to live because of the clean air, the altitude and the awesome beauty.

Yet there is a more significant attraction for the vast majority who flock to Sedona. They are New Agers, and they find, in the words of Dick Sutphen*, a well known New Age author and hypnotist who knows the area, "an undeniable spiritual vibration emanating throughout the

* "Sedona: Psychic Energy Vortexes" by Dick Sutphen (Valley of the Sun Publishing, Box 38, Malibu, CA 90265 - 1986).

54

area." For me I recognised only the beauty and the fairyland symmetry of bell shaped rocks and changing colours with the movement of the sun. And I recognised a lot of deceived New Agers. Though once a New Ager, I was neither troubled nor aware of the "extraordinary energy" that, according to Sutphen, is felt by every person who wanders through the canyons. Yet Sutphen's book can be helpful to our discernment for it describes what is the reality for the New Agers. Perhaps they do indeed experience that "the psychic energy (in Sedona) is greater than anywhere else in the country."

Science doesn't afford any basis for these energies. I know some New Agers would be aware of these energies; I am not. New Age experience is New Age reality! When, as a New Ager, I walked over the Lomond hills of Scotland with thirty others, all carrying a dowsing (or divining) pendulum, the violent swing of the ball on the end of the string would indicate the powerful energy spots. All of the pendula of the entire group turned in a similar fashion. This was our confirmation. This was our experience. Yet I can say as a Christian that demonic forces were at work. We were all deceived. Demonic forces were at work with the New Agers as they reached out for their personal experiences on the high ground surrounding Sedona.

On our expeditions in Scotland we used to say the best energy spots, important as places to build a house or to meditate, were where the ley-lines crossed. In other words the crossing of two energy lines multiplied the energy given out from the earth at that point. Indeed many old churches standing today, were built on the old pagan temple sites at points where people steeped in occult legend dowsed and drew the lines. It is true that straight lines can be drawn between major sites across Britain, and many, even Christians, seek to thus prove the existence of ley-lines. What we have are sites on lines simply because of direction given for building that way, by demons. In pagan times the question wasn't by Christians to Almighty God: "Where shall we build our church?" or "Where shall we dig for water?" The question was put by earth worshippers to Mother Earth, with the demons answering in a variety of ways, perhaps in response to the dowsing rod, still widely used for water divining today.

Understanding Sedona!

We remember to keep in mind that Satan and his demons cannot be trusted; also Satan can masquerade as an angel of light (2 Corinthians 11:14). We need to note the following as an aid to understanding Sedona and the so-called energy vortexes to be found there:

1. Men are deceived when they *do* find water with a divining rod or pendulum. They are deceived because they act contrary to God's Word which forbids divination: *"Let no-one be found among you who sacrifices his son or daughter in the fire, who practises divination or sorcery, interprets omens, engages in witchcraft, or casts spells, or who is a medium or spiritist or who consults the dead"*
(Deuteronomy 18:10-11).

2. Because divination is used to find water that plainly *does* exist it *doesn't* follow that the so-called energy found by dowsing *does* exist. In fact it *does not*.

3. If this energy is supposed to exist, how can it be that Christians do not locate it, and only those in Satan's kingdom find it? The answer is that it is a deception.

In Sedona they didn't speak of crossing leylines but of vortexes, and to explain the deception, Sutphen uses another deception, acupressure, but the analogy is clear. There are many vortexes on the earth and they are compared to the acupressure points on the human body. Although there are many vortexes, there are supposed to be very few "major vortex areas". He tells us that Sedona is considered one of the major areas because there are four powerful ones. "In fact," he says, "there are more vortexes concentrated in Sedona than any other area on earth. This probably explains the intense psychic vibrations in the entire area." The cover of Sutphen's book, the main work* on Sedona, tells us also that Sedona is the primary "positive" centre lying on a ley-line connecting to Stonehenge and the two negative power

* "Sedona: Psychic Energy Vortexes" by Dick Sutphen.

spots: the Bermuda Triangle and Sussex County, England. I pray none of our readers in Sussex or elsewhere be tempted to believe or investigate any of these deceptions.

Before we leave Sutphen, let us note his view of the New Age. Self-help is important, anything from subliminal aid in dieting to realising psychic abilities like telepathy. The key is that we create our own reality so that we are not the victim but exert control over life. The Bible tells us, *"He that trusteth in his own heart is a fool"* (Proverbs 28:26), but the responsibility, Sutphen tells us, is ours, and the answers lie within, not in some code like the Bible! However, Sutphen's is a useful view of the New Age, to give us an understanding of the New Ager and his deception.

Let us turn briefly to another New Age booklet, "The Sedona Vortex Experience"* for another reminder of what New Agers seek in Sedona. It is what they seek at Findhorn, in Tibet, in the Baca Grande, and eventually wherever they are. They seek what is really a counterfeit of the Holy Spirit; they seek the "energy" that directs not to the truth of God's Word, but to experience and a focus upon self: "... we can begin to open ourselves up to receive new energy bliss, and ecstasy by aligning with the natural flows of movement in the universe." The booklet purposes to offer guidelines to assist in using this energy not only to deepen our own experience but "to help heal our Earth Mother."

Crystals

I never before saw so many rock crystals as were to be found in Sedona - in the shops, worn around the neck and deposited around the hillside. In "Rock Crystal - the Magic Stone"** we read, "Metaphysically, the rock crystal has been esteemed for many thousands of years as a heaven sent talisman. Since the early days of civilisation, natural quartz crystals have carried the tradition of having mysterious, or even magical properties." There are chapters on "Crystal Gazing", rock crystal used in a pendulum, "Healing with

* "The Sedona Vortex Experience" by Gayle Johansen and Shinan Naom Barclay (Sunlight Productions, P.O. Box 1300, Sedona, AZ 86336 - 1987).

** Compiled and Edited by Korra Deaver, PhD (Samuel Weiser Inc. Box 612, York Beach, Maine 03910 - 1985).

Crystals" and "Meditation with Crystals." In "The New Age Catalogue"* we read that "Quartz crystals represent perfected material form, aligned and harmonised with the cosmic force. They are much like the pyramids in that they channel high frequency energy onto the physical earth plane."

Thus we are not surprised to find crystals as part of the equipment at Sedona. It all helps to support the deception! Yet let us not think any of these things are peculiar only to remote parts of America. We can go to Glastonbury, and whilst the scene there may appear different, Christian discernment reveals the same deceptions. What we have in Sedona is NOT an energy centre but an outstandingly beautiful part of God's earth, and apart from that it is no different from any other place.

Yet the New Ager network of Sedona is like a webb that catches flies if they put a foot wrong. It is true I would not encourage the unsaved to go there and risk being caught up in the evangelism of the New Age. *"The way of the wicked is as darkness: they know not at what they stumble"* (Proverbs 4:19). Yet for Christians in Sedona and elsewhere, what an opportunity there is to witness to those who seek spiritual truth, what an opportunity there is to proclaim the truth from God's word: *"and there is no God else beside me; a just God and a Saviour; there is none beside me. Look unto me, and be ye saved, all the ends of the earth; for I am God, and there is none else"* (Isaiah 45:21-22).

Then back to Boulder, Colorado - The New Age Mecca

Apart from hearing the name on cowboy films at the cinema, I had never heard of Boulder, as I made my way from England to Denver and the Baca Grande. Colorado is a very large state with a very small population. It has high mountains, American Indian traditions, and a past that evidences tolerance of the occult. As early as 1946 a columnist for the "Rocky Mountain News" wrote "I am

* "The New Age Catalogue - Access to Information and Sources" by the editors of "Body, Mind and Spirit" (Doubleday, New York - 1988).

58

proud rather than regretful that Denver is a city of cults.''

That is at the root of what I found in Colorado. The ''Denver Self-Discovery Expo'' was in progress while I was there and the King Rameses II (Egypt 1279 to 1213 B.C.) exhibition just closing had broken all records for the Denver Museum. I travelled from Denver to Boulder a few times and made two stays there. Here was truly a 1988 Mecca of the New Age. I had heard of the mass meditation across the world on 31st. December 1986. I knew also about the similar world-wide event in August 1987; I remembered passing by Glastonbury at the time of the event and I picked up a leaflet for it which highlighted Boulder. Yet it was only when I unexpectedly found myself in Boulder that I realised the significance of the place. These two across-the-globe events, the World Instant of Cooperation and the Harmonic Convergence, had been organised from Boulder. Like Sedona, but much bigger, here was a town overrun by New Agers, the nerve centre of these and of other international outreaches.

With a population of 80,000 the town at first sight looked like many others. Yet I found that a great many of the shops in the popular town centre malls were New Age. In one shop window I read ''They're here... crystals energised in the Great Pyramid.'' One news feature very aptly described Boulder as ''a spiritual supermarket.'' It went on, ''I'd be surprised if there were another town that sold more crystals or held more psychic consultations per capita. I've even heard the boys at Ray's pub, the working class men's bar off 30th Street, arguing over such intangibles as reincarnation, channeling and the Tarot. Here spirituality rivals only the weather and the Broncos, it seems, as conversation fodder.'' That describes Boulder exactly! There is no doubt that Boulder leaves a lasting impression!

''New Frontiers''*, a so-called magazine of transformation, described Boulder as ''A New Age Mecca.'' Just like Sedona, the idea of the energy is the key to Boulder's success. Legend has it that an underground parabolic arc of over a billion tons of quartz crystal makes it a ''unique locale

* Rocky Mountain Edition P.O. Box 8005, Suite 390, Boulder, CO 80306-8005.

for psychic sending and receiving and other energy work."

The truth is that deceived people, in this case New Agers congregating in one place, fuel the deception by their evangelism and the unity that exists among them. The deceptions in Boulder, dangers for the undiscerning and the unwary, are a function of the evil and the idolatry found in the hearts of men; they have nothing whatever to do with crystals or with the geology and geography of Boulder.

Boulder has much to commend it, not only its beauty but, as the report confirms, it has "amenities such as safe streets." Important in the context here, Boulder has more successful and grounded New Age activity than any other town in North America. I had visited Los Angeles, California and knew of its reputation with New Agers. I know of London. Yet unlike the big metropolis, in Boulder the New Age is concentrated. The population of the whole of the state of Colorado is but a handful compared to Los Angeles. If Colorado is the New Age centre of the world, Boulder is its capital!

As if to emphasise the importance of my own discoveries in Colorado, no soon had I returned when I received a copy of the latest "New York Times Magazine" (1st May 1988) which ran a lengthy feature on "Colorado's Thriving Cults." Then our own "Guardian" newspaper (3rd June 1988) carried the headline "New Age tentacles dig deep into Colorado." Let Alex Brummer's report from Boulder in the "Guardian" describe one individual's enterprise involving New Age nonsense where one evidently successful New Ager is doing his own thing! He's an individualist yet the mix is the same! Improve the vibrations (the energy), improve the meditation and put the crystals to work!

"High in the pine covered Rocky Mountain foothills above Boulder, Greg Hoag sits in his bedroom beneath a bronze 3-D Star sculpture loaded with gemstones and crystals, as he sips herb tea.

Greg, a youthful 40-year-old looks across the round, pine coffee table in front of him where a glistening collection of quartz crystals, gems and stones are displayed and talks enthusiastically of his latest creation "a matrix of 100 crossed bronze diamonds and 200 magnets conforming to a DNA pattern,'' which underlays the mattress on his pink painted bed.

Like the other devices created by Greg's company, Metaforms, including giant bronze pyramids used for meditation, the bed board is designed to enhance vibrational qualities, open the body Chakras (or energy centres) and ''harmonise the mind body and spirit.'' For good measure it has also ''improved our sex lives,'' he confirms.

Greg and his wife, Gail, who built an affluent hot-tub life-style making and selling leather cowboy belts to tourists, are among thousands of entrepreneurs, teachers, spiritualists, holistic medical pratitioners and pyshic astrologists who have helped transform Colorado - and Boulder in particular - into a magnet for what has become known as the New Age.''

Unlike the Baca Grande, Boulder already had its Tibetans fifteen years ago. The ''New York Times Magazine'' article observes that so rapidly do fashions of the spirit change in Boulder that, by comparison to some, the Tibetan Buddhist Naropa Institute seems as staid as the *Episcopal* Church. Yet I don't know if the man from the Times saw the brochure ''Serpent Power'' available in Boulder. The goal of this group is to promote ''the occult sciences as legitimate and respectable disciplines for serious psychological and spiritual growth,'' my own desire when I started delving deeper and deeper into the occult. However, in Boulder, I noted at which church the classes were held. They were to be held at St. John's *Episcopal* Church! In the *''Pyramid* Chapel''!

Then there's the Boulder-based Rocky Mountain Spiritual Emergence Network. They offer support services for individuals who hear inner voices, those who get a sense of past experience or who experience ''profound estrangement'' from the material world. All these things are not seen as causes for alarm but as part of a material process of spiritual unfoldment. Yet Christian concern can only increase as we find the board president of the Boulder County Health Department and the nurse manager of Boulder Community Hospital's medical psychiatric unit among the Network's directors.

5

Occult Nature of the New Age Movement

The Occult and Human Potential

"A woman sat in a darkened room and accurately described the exact layout of a top secret military base four hundred miles away - which she had never seen before.

She claimed to be "seeing" it through the eyes of a man at the base by tuning into his mind.

The thirty-five year old woman also read out the numbers of several parked cars - all of which were later traced to workers at the base.

*And she even "heard" the pilot of a naval plane landing at the base giving important flight details to the control tower."**

This is not the script of the latest "Star Wars" film. It is a serious report in the London "Daily Star". It is not just one of the thousands of ordinary reports of psychic experiences that are found in every newspaper. According to the "Daily Star" this took place in the Pentagon, the nerve centre of America's war machine, and it was organised by an undercover team of U.S. Government scientists experimenting with "mindpower." However in these days it is not uncommon to read stories where mindpower is used in national and international business. Whether we call it "mindpower" or psychic power, what

* London "Daily Star". Used by permission.

we are talking about is Man's so-called human potential, beyond the natural realm which everyone understands. We are reading about occult power, and it is to be found in the area of the military, in government, in business, in medicine and in every area of life.

The New Age has introduced more and more to astrology, yoga, spiritism, divination, mind-control techniques and much else that Christians are today recognising as occult. The ground has been prepared. More and more police departments, government departments or any other department running the affairs of men will have staff eager to bring in the methods of the New Age.

What Christians need to grasp is that there is nothing remarkable about the stories they read in the newspapers where the works of the devil are concerned. They may be mis-reported but it would be a mistake not to see clearly the signs of the fast-developing one-world government and religion of our own day.

For our examples of demons working through people in an ever more significant way, stay with what the London "Daily Star" had to say about the Russian end of the "Mindwar"! One top Russian psychic scientist reports regularly on the progress of her former colleagues. "Anything is possible with the mind. Anything", she said. It is true, for once given access to an open and willing mind demons can gain a right of entry all the more certainly as the person persists in the forbidden practices that are an abomination to God. The scientist relates that as part of her training to move satellites off course by the power of the mind, one Moscow housewife used the power to suspend objects in the air. While she concentrates, objects rise from the floor and remain motionless in the air for minutes at a time. These must not be seen as a sort of conjuring trick; it is demon-power. This housewife has been encouraged to open her mind to the supernatural destructive purposes of Satan. Natural man can recognise the evil of murder and even the evils of satellite warfare but there is more than that in the Bible. In the last chapter but one, we read:

But the fearful, and unbelieving, and the abominable,

63

and murderers, and whoremongers, and sorcerers, and idolaters, and all liars, shall have their part in the lake which burneth with fire and brimstone: which is the second death. (Revelation 21:8).

The scientist reported on another who can stop animals in their tracks and cause bodily harm to human beings. One researcher who strayed into her line of vision during an experiment sustained the sort of injury that only a laser beam could otherwise cause. As the researcher's eye happened to catch the subject's while she was staring across the room it was badly burned making necessary major surgery of the retina. Christian missionaries in Africa, familiar with the power of curses to bring about death in those places, will have no difficulty with such reports. Times have changed but the ways of demons with those who have opened themselves up to the occult have not.

Of course the signs of the times in the area of the New Age, from Alternative Medicine through to Zen involves a formidable list. In the list that follows we include cults and areas of occult that can often provide the clue to New Age activity. The list can assist in recall of any past involvement and where identification and repentance is necessary.

We caution here that not every heading given need be necessarily occult. An example is the sort of "handwriting analysis" used by the police; this is perfectly acceptable but the occult version is not. Our purpose throughout is to encourage the reader in his own discernment. The list is not intended as a basis for further extensive research into the areas listed, but the Holy Spirit is the communicator and He can use this list to prompt a reminder, or to prompt further enquiry into what a son, or a daughter, or a friend, may be involved in that might not be right. We purposefully don't make this an alphabetical list. We suggest no order or logic, only that the list may be helpful to bring matters to mind - perhaps even occult areas not listed here but which may be prompted by another reference.

1. Occult

Hatha Yoga
Cartomancy
Fortune telling
Palmistry
Charms
Birth signs
Pentagrams
Ouija boards
Levitation
Automatic writing
Clairvoyance
Clairaudience
Divination
Telepathy
Superstitions
Mind control
Psychic powers
Pendulum swinging
Table tipping
Handwriting analysis
Hallowe'en
Akashic records
Almanac
Age of Aquarius
Aquarian gospel
Soul travel
Horoscopes
Atlantis
Aura
Taboos
Amulets
Dream interpretation
Exorcism
ESP
Rudolf Steiner
Intuitive arts counselling
Phrenology

Magic (black & white)
Reincarnation
Spiritism
Tarot cards
Spells
Hypnosis
Osiris
'Dungeons and Dragons'
Astral travel
Taekwondo
Taoism
Mushindo karate
Aikido
T'ai Chi Ch'uan
Karate
Hapkido
Wu Shu
Spirit combat
Feng-sao
Dowsing
Soothsayers
Augury
Automatic drawing
Devil dancing
Fetishes
Firewalking
Hexagrams
Omens
Telekinesis
Mesmerism
Autosuggestion
Cabbala
Mascots
Numerology
Incantations
Talismans
Fantasy role-playing games

Card cutting	Card reading
Hand reading	Psychoanalysis
Teacup reading	
Rod divination	Freud
Seances	'Holy' objects
Martial arts	AMORC
Judo	Oriental ornaments
Ju-jitsu	Addictions
Ch'uan-fa	Spoon bending
Kung-fu	Voices in the mind
Weeping Statues	Counterfeit Tongues
Standing stones	Evil eye
Ley lines	Electric shock treatment
Religious idols	Nanbudo
Church pagan connections	Water divining
Graphology	Mirror mantic
Incubus	Kissing of idols
Succubus	Glass moving
Parapsychology	Idols
Psycho-cybernetics	Teraphims
UFO's	Stargazing
Yoga	Old Moore
Charming	Stonehenge
Curses (*by* you or *on* you)	Demonised souvenirs
Lucky charms	Buddhas
Kabala	Swastika
Tribal dancing	Images (frogs, cats, owls,
Astral projection	bats and night creatures
Candle staring	used in witchcraft)
Drugs	Indian elephants
Ghosts	Pyramids
Pagan celebrations	Obelisks
Gipsy curse	Serpents
Psychokinesis (PK)	Witch markings
Zodiac signs	Myths
I Ching	Fairies and pixies
Moving Statues	Unbiblical Mass

2. Cults

Anglo-Israelism
The Worldwide Church of God
Baha'ism
Black Muslims
Christian Science
Conceptology
Freemasons and other secret societies
I AM
Inner Peace Movement
Lourdes
Madonna and Child
Spiritualism
Swedenborgianism
Theosophical Society
Unitarianism
Unity School of Christianity
Universalism
Ultimate reconciliation
Voodoo
Witchcraft
Zen Buddhism
Marxism
Moral Rearmament
Astrology
Human Potential Movement
Children of God
Hare Krishna
Gurdjieff
Baba-lovers
Sufi
Fatima
Roman Catholicism
Divine Light Mission
Christadelphianism
Jehovah's Witnesses
Modernism, liberalism and the social gospel
Mormonism
New Thought
Rosicrucianism
Satanism
Scientology
Seventh Day Adventism
Spiritual Frontiers Fellowship
Saints
Medugorje
Communism
Buffaloes
Islam (Mohammedism)
Hinduism
Buddhism
Humanism
Eastern ceremonial dances
Pagan customs
Shrines
Pagan tourist places
Subud
Shepherding/Discipleship
Moonies
Unification Church
Anthroposophy
'Star Wars'
Theosophy
False philosophies
Belief systems
Mary worship
Eckankar
Walsingham
Est
Personal growth movement
Mind dynamics

The Healing Movement
Cooneyites
False religions
Druids
Transcendental
  Meditation

Erhard Seminars Training
The Aquarian Gospel
Zoroastrianism
Family of Love
The Way

3. Holistic Healing Therapies

N.B. — Further explanations are to be found in "Understanding Alternative Medicine - Holistic Health in the New Age" (3rd. Edition) - New Wine Press.

Astrologic Medicine
Acupuncture
Auriculotherapy
Acupressure
Moxibustion
Jin Shin Do
Reflexology
Polarity Therapy
Yoga
T'ai Chi
Aikido
Mushindo Karate
Shiatsu
Anthroposophical medicine
Bach Flower Remedies
Herbal concoctions
Hakims
Ginseng
Osteopothy
Chiropractic
Naturopathy
Touch-for-Health
Reiki programme
Biopathy
Alexander method
Breathing therapy
Air therapy
Earth therapy

Biorhythms
Hypnotherapy
Hypnosis
Self-hypnosis tapes
Meditation
Contemplative Prayer
Auto-Suggestion
Couéism
Visualisation therapy
Mind Control
Quieting Reflex
Passivity
Centering
Guided imagery
Chromotherapy
Biofeedback
The Placebo
Psychotherapy
Psychoanalysis
Autogenics
Dream therapy
Aversion therapy
Metamorphic technique
Primal therapy
Inner healing
Rogerian therapy
Encounter therapy
Gestalt

Holonomic integration breathing

Rebirthing

Tissue salts therapy

Holistic cosmetics

Bates eyesight training

Sound therapies

Aromatherapy

Macrobiotics

Zone therapy

Orgonomy (Reichian Therapy)

Bio-energetics

Do-in

Feldenkrais technique

Rolfing

Mora therapy

Orthobionomy

Behavioural Kinesiology

Bio-kinesiology

Christian Science

Past Lives therapy

Psychic diagnosis

Radiesthesia

Clairvoyance

Clairaudience

Inherited powers

Pendulum divination

Radionics

Psychometry

Kirlian photography

Palmistry

Mediumistic Iridology

Homoeopathy

Psychodrama

Transactional analysis

Co-counselling

Clinical theology

Transpersonal psychology

Psychosynthesis

Group dynamics

Group psychotherapy

Interpersonal relationship

Positive thinking

Positive confession

Positive mental attitude

Human potential movement

Spiritualist healing

Psychic healing

Faith healing

Absent healing

Hand healers

Magnetic healing

Healing with magnets

Psychic surgery

Witchdoctors

Shamans

Charming of warts

Copper bracelets

Crystal therapy

Pattern therapy

Pyramid healing

Ayurveda

Therapeutic touch

Applied Kinesiology

Psionic medicine

That is a formidable list of areas that may, in one manner or another, open the door to the occult. Let us not take a wholly intellectual viewpoint and trouble ourselves unduly about whether an item should be listed or not. Items could have been omitted to satisfy the intellectual mind! However I believe this would have made the list less useful.

Never a Coincidence!

There is much in Satan's armoury we do not *fully* understand; let us not doubt the power and language of symbol and ritual among the initiated. The pyramid is such a symbol and it is no coincidence that "the pyramids" are found in Egypt. The pyramid was a symbol representing the unknown and nameless deity in pre-Christian cults. They have even appeared on a series of Vatican stamps. Pyramids appear these days, seemingly pointlessly, in the advertising displays of major corporations. It is no coincidence for example that the Celtic pagan festival of Beltane was celebrated wherever possible on hills pyramidical in shape. It is no coincidence that the pyramid (with the all-seeing eye) appears on every U.S. One Dollar bill. It is not a coincidence that the date on that pyramid is 1776, though admittedly the date of America's independence is in that year. More significantly May 1st 1776 was the day of the founding of the Order of the Illuminati.

More central still is the Church of Rome. Yet there is a big role too for the United Nations. The world may seem to be in the hands of the politicians who go to the United Nations in New York, but those who have the international financial and occult power to manipulate events for one-world government are the ones to watch. We are witnessing in our day, not only the rapid advancement of ecumenism and unity with various religious faiths, but also the "Novus Ordo Seclorum" ("New World Order"). We see it written around the pyramid and the all-seeing eye on the U.S. Dollar bill. The United Nations *is* a vital part. The New Order is political, social *and* religious, and we see the hand of Rome reaching in.

Man in his unredeemed state has a conscience, which leads him to seek what he knows in his heart is still lacking. Many are sincere seekers in what they do, yet without Jesus

Christ can have no real direction. In these days of great wealth and opportunity for those who have "made it" according to the world's view, there is little left for them except to look outside the world of material things. The London "Sunday Express Magazine" 18th November 1984 featured an interview with the then Saudi Arabian billionaire Adnan Khashoggi. The interviewer asked about one of his projects to build a pyramid in Egypt. Mr Khashoggi replied: "...A glass pyramid surrounded by an artificial lake with a museum and leisure centre. It's not happened because archaeologists fear the lake would affect the real pyramids." The pyramids in Egypt are a centre of occult power and an abomination to the Lord, a link in time between Babylon and Rome.

The Peace Symbol and Witchcraft

The occult is never far away when Man's fantasies or New Age ideas get on their way. Most will be familiar with news reports of protest against nuclear weapons which is perfectly logical to the mind of natural Man. As a member of a CND group I found the old-hands in CND more committed in their singular task than the politicians and even the average committed Christian. The Campaign becomes their god. They are zealous for their cause and, without realising it, they open themselves up to further attention from Satan's spiritual realm. The English CND Festival in 1985 was held at Glastonbury, a place like Sedona, Arizona well understood by occultists as a centre for spiritual power.

In the past thirty years or so we have seen the introduction of many occult symbols into the jewellery worn by both men and women. A most important symbol introduced in the same way is one known as the "Peace Symbol". For hundreds of years it has been known in witchcraft as the broken cross.

Professing as a man of peace, and after Vatican II, Pope Paul VI brought into use the symbol of the Broken Cross.

71

Piers Compton, in his book "The Broken Cross"* tells us that few present day Catholics are aware of the meaning of the symbol, and underneath one of the revealing photographic plates in this book we read the caption: "Pope John Paul II displays the sinister symbol of the bent or broken cross showing the repulsive and distorted figure of Christ invented by Satanists in the fifth century, and used by black magicians and sorcerers in the Middle Ages to represent the Biblical term 'mark of the beast.'"

As we examine the New Age we shall see the occult at every turn. I believe the purpose of the New Age is to bring individuals into that realm, making them receptive to the plans their leaders have for them. The "Peace Symbol" is simply another way to keep people in Satan's bondage and rulership. The truth is that the "Peace Symbol" is not what the world believes.

The "Peace Symbol" is a sign of the times. It does not have the meaning its wearers give to it. Let us discern the signs of the times:

"And when ye see the south wind blow, ye say, There will be heat; and it cometh to pass. Ye hypocrites, ye can discern the face of the sky and of the earth; but how is it that ye do not discern this time?" (Luke 12:55-56)

On our journey we shall see different signposts. My purpose throughout this book is to present the signposts I can see.

Fantasy: Road to the Occult

Any chapter on the occult can go on for ever. The subjects are endless. Fantastic stories become even more fantastic, and not because of exaggeration. Can statues be made to weep? Of course they can. Can some pictures be accursed things? Certainly they can. Can a man ever demolish a house with his bare hand? Yes he can. Demons can operate in all of these areas and in thousands more. An idol is an abomination to the Lord and some, if they are themselves open to the work of demons as they gaze upon it, may well

* published by Neville Spearman, Jersey - 1983

see it weep. Those who open their minds may well succeed in things of the mind over things of matter. Karate and the Martial Arts come into this category, and again we witness what Man calls his human potential.

What we need to remember is that all Satan's ways have a great deal in common. They are made possible in the lives of those who have opened their minds to the activities of demons by disregarding God's Word and God's warnings about things which are an abomination to Him (Deuteronomy 18:12). We find throughout the occult realm the counterfeit of what the Holy Spirit desires to do.

We find Man falling into the same trap that the serpent set for Eve. We even see in the occult realm many who are finding it easy to draw a line between what they see as "good" spirits and "bad". They are being used by demons who even counterfeit the discernment that God requires of His people. In these days, men speak of God who do not *know* God.

Narnia

Men can go off the track. Perhaps Solomon was one of the first, for inspired as his writings are in our Bible, his other writings are important in the Witchcraft Bible where his words on how to conjure demons can be found.

No man's writings can be endorsed apart from what is in the Word of God. Among the prolific writers, who is there that is 100% free from error? C.S. Lewis is readily quoted as an authority by Christian writers, yet we can look at his writing line by line, word by word. Leaving aside any esoteric meaning in the C.S. Lewis Narnia series of books written for children, what of the following dialogue from "Prince Caspian"?

"Sweet Master Doctor, learned Master Doctor, who ever heard of a witch that really died? You can always get them back. "Call her up," said the grey voice, "We are all ready. Draw the circle. Prepare the blue fire."

Children learn protection against Satan's devices from

* from "Prince Caspian", C.S. Lewis 1951, published by Collins

God's Word and not the doctrines of demons. What is good for children is found only in the Word of God. Fantasy opens the door to the occult and even where the occult isn't dished up to them directly, Satan can seize on fantasies which are often so vivid in a child's mind. They are receptive to the occult just at the age which God purposes as the easiest time to begin a relationship with an unseen Jesus. The god of this world knows the best time to take control in the lives of the children of Christians and others. Parents need to heed the word of Paul who said, *"For your obedience is come abroad unto all men. I am glad therefore on your behalf: but yet I would have you wise unto that which is good, and simple concerning evil"* (Romans 16:19).

Discernment is vital and many Christians seem to have practically no discernment at all! One Christian woman who had a Christian home wrote to me in this way about her experiences as a child.

From the age of eight to thirteen I spent most of my free time reading and dreaming about Narnia. Over that period I read each Chronicle seven times and kept a notebook of comments I found helpful, much like one would with a Bible.

Through the years Aslan came to mean as much to me as Jesus. I had a map of Narnia in my bedroom and I drew great comfort by gazing into the solemn face of Aslan featured on it.

I spent much time attempting to find a way into Narnia by pleading with Aslan to let me in, or willing myself through paintings or backs of wardrobes, or attempting to converse with my pet rabbit in case she knew a secret route!

I had been told that Aslan represented Jesus, but instead of this encouraging me to know the Lord better I was drawn into further mystical, magical and occult reading. After I became a Christian my theology remained somewhat confused by my Narnian background as I had believed the story to be a literal allegory of the Gospel when in fact it was not.

I feel that my interest in, and eventual obsession with

Narnia was neither a helpful nor healthy heritage to my Christian life.

"Buzz" magazine used some perhaps unwittingly appropriate language in the article "God's Lion of Literature."

...Lewis has attracted a CULT following .... Youngsters ENCHANTED by his Narnia series of books write to Lewis asking for more .... The remarkable man who used lions, witches and wardrobes to CHARM children and intelllectuals to the faith. (My emphasis.)*

Yes his work had a magnetic appeal to the Rev. Walter Hooper, Lewis's Secretary. Asked if this was the appeal to Lewis's work that made people want to read more and more of his books, Hooper answered:

Yes. Once you have read one of his books, you just have to read another and another. I first read Lewis when I was at university and I was so overwhelmed that I went into bookshops and asked for anything by this man. And from the letters I get, that seems to be true with a great many people. There hasn't been a day in the past twenty-six years when I haven't read some of his work.*

Real Space Men?

A question and answer programme was seen on television in December 1985.** The questioners were youngsters from the studio audience and, being questioned were self-styled "Star-persons" from the constellation Orion. It was explained to the children, who were admittedly bright and sceptical, that there would be a mass evacuation of people in the near future, known as the 'Rapture' in Christian teaching. What we had was a very serious programme laced with many aspects of the occult - biokinesiology as used by chiropractors and homoeopaths, ley-lines, UFO's, kirlian photography, the return of the rainbow warrior, hand-crafted bracelets to help the body's so called auric field,

* "Buzz" Magazine — August 1979
** "Open to Question" (BBC 2) 10th December 1985

and all the rest. The programme went a long way towards putting together a New Age jigsaw that made a great deal of sense to natural minds already programmed with much existing material. Even the Rothschilds and the Rockefellers got a mention! We were told they were responsible for much of the covering-up there had been up to this time. Our children were presented with a comprehensive picture right down to the explanation they can use if left behind in the Rapture. The programme was in effect introducing children unsuspectingly to New Age thinking. How cruel Satan is! What a mix up! What confusion is sown!

"Opening The Door to the Unknown Guest"

The "guest", if only the writer of those title words knew it, is a demon, and the above is the headline to a half-page story* that landed on my breakfast table in 1987. I read that a famous Swiss banking firm had recently taken to dowsing on the Stock Exchange and that several Japanese firms employ spirit mediums as consultants. I knew there was a relatively new Koestler Chair of Parapsychology at Edinburgh University with a role on the clinical side, and now I read of the Koestler Foundation and how it had been pulling in hard-headed businessmen for its seminars on the "irrational areas of what it calls the ecology of the mind."

"Sir John Harvey Jones, former chairman of I.C.I ... headed an attendance list that united Shell and B.P., Saatchi and Saatchi and Coopers and Lybrand, and even included a representative from one of the research councils which dispense government cash to scientists."

Opening the door to the unknown guest is the bottom line in all of these programmes. We are told that the term was coined by Maurice Maeterlinck, a Nobel laureate, not because he recognised the demonic opportunities and the altered states of consciousness that open them up; rather

* "Daily Telegraph" London Friday Matters (7th August 1987)

76

they described the "invisible prompter" who seemed, through dreams or hunches or sudden bursts of inspiration, to be jogging the elbows of creative giants like Einstein, Kipling and Jung. By 1988 executives in our own public services sector were caught up with the New Age. The stage is past when it is mainly the captains of industry, the individualists and the leading thinkers who are involved with the New Age. One Electricity Board executive who attended a course on "New Age Thinking - for achieving your potential," showed me his course tapes and files. The following are some of the subject headings: New Age Thinking; How our Self-Image is formed; Possibility Thinking - Expanding your Awareness; New Age Thinking - the Challenge is Yours; Affirmations and Visualisation."

Visualisation is a very powerful tool of the occult. First the idea is to affirm, and if you affirm with faith, and keep affirming, it may come to pass. Yet it is not God's faith. When New Agers visualise - a more powerful practice than simply affirming - the visions or visualisations do not come from God. When they are confirmed, or when they work, or when they help, it may seem that they do! Yet, in business, as elsewhere where the Devil is let in, Satan can masquerade as an angel of light (2 Corinthians 11:14). The question is not "does it work?" The question for those who care about their eternal destinations is "where does the power come from?" For those who care and for all those who don't believe, as Christians we can pray. We must shut out the occult and so keep the door closed against the unknown and invisible guest (Isaiah 8:19-20).

Star Wars: Now Beyond the Fantasy Stage

In the United States in 1985 I was shown a recruitment film of the U.S. Military. Yet it wasn't any ordinary invitation to any ordinary military branch. This was a film introduced by a senior uniformed officer in the U.S. Military and describing the work of the First Earth Batallion. Couched in esoteric language, this was a film about the occult operations of America's war effort. Another film, this time a TV documentary, was specifically devoted to what is officially called Satanic Crime. I watched the operations of one U.S. Police Department in combatting this sort of crime. The Department had been formed for that purpose. In the Psychiatry Departments of hospitals doctors are being addressed by demons who they don't recognise in their patients. Men need to know that exposure to the ways of the devil places them in danger whatever their situation. Researchers are in danger too. Satan's hidden mysteries should stay hidden. Students study parapsychology in these new departments of our universities at their peril. The Bible is very clear:

There shall not be found among you any one that maketh his son or his daughter to pass through the fire, or that useth divination, or an observer of times, or an enchanter, or a witch.

Or a charmer, or a consulter with familiar spirits, or a wizard or a necromancer.

For all that do these things are an abomination unto the Lord. (Deuteronomy 18:10-12).

How many have, as they believe, tuned their "human potential" to the point where they can walk through embers barefoot without ill effects? There are many in these days. On one evening 40 barefoot participants strode through an eight foot pit of burning embers with a temperature of 1,300 degrees Fahrenheit and none suffered more than the odd blister.*

Is it surprising that with capabilities like these Man gains a confidence that is not his own, a supernatural potential that Satan will continue to exploit, blinding those involved to the things of God and the truth of His word? Man is being ever more indoctrinated in the New Age. Not only are unredeemed men being well-prepared, they are being organised too. They are being fitted into Satan's schemes, both in the Pentagon and the Kremlin. Yet there are others

---

* reported in "Daily Telegraph" (26-11-84)

whom Satan is using in his attempt to rule the world in the short time that remains to him.

Satan Counterfeits Everything!

Satan's wiles are not in any sense straightforward (Genesis 3:1). All the complexities of the world's institutions and all of the deceived hearts and minds of sinful men are available to him. Whichever way we turn we find the key to be occult practices of every kind. There is such a mixture to deceive the world, yet the Lord makes it so simple when given Deuteronomy 18:10-12 as previously quoted and a good dictionary for those who find some of the words unfamiliar.

In every branch of the occult the story is the same. Satan seeks to counterfeit everything which God can do. Whatever is done in the power of the Holy Spirit, demons, where God allows, can produce the counterfeit. As Christians we can hear what the Holy Spirit is saying. The spiritualist, believing he is hearing from the spirits of the dead, hears what the demons tell him. Those in the occult realm sit in yoga or meditation, and as they empty their minds or focus on a Hindu mantra, the opportunity is given to demons to increase whatever hold has already been given. The effect seems to be cumulative and we only have to look at the stories of individuals to see how occult bondage can become stronger and stronger.

As Christians meditating upon the Word of God, we can hear what the Holy Spirit is saying to us through the Word (Joshua 1:8; Psalms 1:2-3; Acts 20:32; Colossians 3:16). If there were more prayerful reading and meditation on, and obedience to, God's Word, there would be less deception. *"The sword of the Spirit, which is the word of God"* (Ephesians 6:17) defeats the enemy of souls and he should be no match for those who know their Bibles.

Symbols and Other Abominations

Treasures, statues, symbols, and all manner of things can be abominations in the sight of God (Deuteronomy 7:26). The Daily Telegraph reported in 1985 up to 10,000 people going each night to Ballinspittle, a village in Ireland following reports of a statue of the Virgin Mary seen to move. Of course idols have moved, of course statues of Mary have been seen to cry. These things are an abomination in the sight of God and, in the manner of the symbols, the Rock music and all the rest, they represent an invitation to demons. Treasures too can come into this category. It was reported in Texas in 1984 that one well-known evangelist was offered a collection of art and other objects from Asia for his ministry. He accepted the gift worth about $1m and was on his way to auction it when he re-read Old Testament verses about destroying graven images. He then returned the collection to the donor, who then destroyed various graven images, temple dogs and other objects, and after a night of destruction threw them in Lake Worth. That is a story with two endings. *First* God will honour the obedience of those who are tested in situations such as that one. *Second* as the world read the story: "Remnants of the collection were retrieved from the lake by a couple who were on a fishing trip; they sent them to auction in Houston where they realised $581!"*

T.V., Fantasy, and Spiritual Music

As king in the occult realm Satan can begin whenever we take our eyes off Jesus. Certainly television presents him with ample opportunity to reach us. People who believe they can control TV viewing are mostly idealistic not realistic. The majority of people would acknowledge their weakness in controlling their viewing. Natural hearts love sin (Mark 7:21-22; John 3:19), ears listen for sin, and eyes look for sin (1 John 2:16). Then who is able to keep sin

* "Daily Telegraph" (5-12-84)

from flashing before them on a screen at any moment? Particularly after owning a TV for any time, can we even *recognise* sin when we see it, either in the programmes or in the advertisements? The effect of being yoked to unbelievers and to sin through the TV screen is to become hardened. What do righteousness and wickedness have in common? (2 Corinthians 6:14-15). The following is a true story from Ontario, Canada:

Approximately, 4 years ago in St. Catherines, Ontario, the newspaper headlines read one day: $500 Paid for Disposing of TV. The article went on to say that a study was done in Detroit in which the goal was to find out to what degree people are controlled by TV. 250 families were scientifically selected from various races and classes to be offered $500 if they would live without their TV set for one month. After 30 days they could take it back in, and receive $500 free. Out of 250, only 50 families agreed to do it. How many families "made it" through this trial of 30 days? Eight! The other 42 forfeited their $500 sometime during the month - one family took their TV back in on the 29th day. The 8 who made it through were interviewed extensively. All eight said it brought their family closer together without TV. Six fathers said they first learned to know their children. One father said: "The day that I disposed of our TV was the first day in 25 years that no one was killed in our living room, no sirens screamed, no shots rang out, no artificial merriment told us when to laugh, and no one slashed anyone else." And what was now the final result of these eight families of whom 7 said their family life was considerably more rewarding without TV? The last line of the article tells us: "All eight families took TV back in." *

But what has television to do with the New Age? The answer is a great deal. It introduces the philosophies of the East into the West and programmes from the West are seen in the East. TV is the focal point in the average home, and in the days to come we shall see many uses lined up for the TV which will make it the more indispensable. In the New

---

* "The Banner of Truth" Tract Mission, 540, Cresent St N.E; Grand Rapids, Michigan 49503 USA

Age it is planned that we pay our bills and buy our airline tickets via our TV terminal. There is much more than computer games planned for the TV in the New Age. In the one-world system, the rulers purpose to make Man dependent on the government. The TV is an important part of that plan.

At least, as Christians, let us consider our case for having TV and let us consider the cost in the spiritual realm before we invite its message into our homes (1 John 2:15). As king in the occult realm, Satan can begin wherever we take our eyes off Jesus. He already began before we were born and the Bible tells of the past generation curses that can be passed down to us, as we are born sinners with the need, from the beginning, to be born again. There should be little room for the fantasy world in which so many youngsters are encouraged to grow up. A conversation with Jesus Christ at bed-time is better than a meditating gaze at a witch on a broomstick swinging in the mobile or a bed-time story of Little Red Riding Hood. Even a more pleasant "Good Night" story can be little better; the good is often the enemy of the best to be found in the Bible, so necessary in the "formative" years.

Then as a teenager, or perhaps many years before, the Christian youngster is introduced to "Christian" Rock music. Once again the demons will be there where the opening is given. Sin gives that opening through the beat familiar to those who have engaged in witchcraft. The strobe lighting in a *"Christian"* disco has the same effect on the mind as the strobe lighting in *any* disco. As a meditator in the occult world where Satan is king I would spend time each day looking into a strobe light. There was not the noise of the disco, but that made no difference. I was tuning up my "human potential". I was emptying my mind just like the kids in the disco, making way for demons to fill it. Music is spiritual and in 1 Samuel 16:23 we can read that when Saul was troubled David played his harp. Saul became well and the demon departed from him. The scripture does not say that David sang; the music itself was sufficient and significant. And so it is with Rock music, quite apart from the words. I believe the Lord will reveal other sorts of music not of Him as we remain open to Him.

We can identify such music both by an *understanding* of Satan's devices and by *discernment*. When I was a "searcher" into the occult realm I used to listen to tapes of waves breaking onto the sea shore. Other times I listened to music with subliminal sounds to give the same result. Such sounds (of the waves or music) were very agreeable. Of course I didn't hear the hidden "subliminal" sounds. However the discerning Christian may recognise, "there's something strange about the music (or that sound); I don't like it." Or we may recognise a hypnotic effect. We can trust the Holy Spirit even when we don't fully understand what the WORD OF GOD is saying; that's discernment. What was actually happening then as I was listening to those waves?

The answer is that beneath the "waves", at a level that is only barely perceptible consciously, the real message is going direct to the seat of all action in your life, your subconscious mind ...... Not knowing where this mind manipulation is at work, it is ever more essential that a person has his mind renewed constantly in the correct way - by THE WORD OF GOD. *

And be not conformed to this world: but be ye transformed by the renewing of your mind, that ye may prove what is that good, and acceptable, and perfect, will of God.' (Romans 12:3)

We look at Rock and New Age Music again, along with more signs of the times in the next chapter.

* "Prophetic Alert" (July 1985) published by Maranatha Revival Crusade, Secunderabad-500 003, A.P.India

6

The Pervasiveness of the New Age

Christians discerning the New Age will come to understand some of the New Age "buzz words". There are many, and one of them is "Global", to suggest a unity to some and a one-world system to others. In 1985 we saw an enormous fund-raising enterprise on behalf of the starving of Ethiopia. The medium used was an international Rock Festival known as "Live Aid". This was applauded by all, Christian and non-Christian alike, and yet the effect of it was to elevate the millionaire Rock super-stars to a significant place both on the New Age scene and in the corridors of government. Even governments dared not ignore their success! The world sees the issue not in terms of the dangers of Rock music in the spiritual realm but in terms of what New Agers see as the conflict between the vested interest of the "Second-Wave" and their own "enlightened" and generous hearts in the New Age, "the Third-Wave", the Age of Aquarius. Here they see a real sensitivity and a sense of urgency to deal with the problems of food, energy, arms control, population, poverty, resources, ecology, climate, the problems of the aged, the breakdown of the urban community, the need for productive and rewarding work, and all the rest. New Agers are prepared to solve these problems in whatever way they can. They go about with zeal.

New Agers dream of a golden age one-world situation, and I myself have as a non-Christian encouraged the firm idea of a one-world government. Certainly we see the move in that direction as the globe gets effectively smaller through speedy communication, travel, and with a focus of human control into fewer and fewer hands. We enlarge further on this scenario in "Understanding the New Age - World Government and World Religion." Yet there is no clear indication from Scripture just how far this will progress. Mankind is rebuilding Babylon, but we do well to remember that the Tower of Babel was never finished. How far will the Lord allow deception to go before He returns?

In the meantime, for many, music is a very significant entry point for the New Age. We do well to look closely at the men, and more especially at their music.

Rock and Occult Music

Elvis Presley was the King of Rock n'Roll. The Beatles are the best known music group of the century. The impact of these musicians has been phenomenal. Indeed Elvis believed he was a prophet and therein lies a clue to the spiritual dimension that Elvis would not deny. He was a False Prophet and things are not what they seem.

Elvis is seen differently depending on the perspective taken. He was a good singer, and certainly he had new music. He was the sex symbol with gyrating hips on stage, but more significantly he was paving the way for the so-called New Morality of the 1960s. They were the swinging sixties. The message was "Anything Goes". Prime Minister MacMillan's words not only applied to the British economy; in the 60s the teenagers - yesterday's "hippies" today's New Age leaders - had "never had it so good."

Both the carefree teenager and the caring but often dismayed Granny well recognise Presley's significance up to that point. But what more was there to Elvis and his music? The important answer is that he was heavily into the occult including the Theosophist/New Age teaching of Madame Blavatsky. He had a personal instructor for Karate, the occult Martial Art, and he was obsessed with death. As a prophet he dispensed various drugs to those around him who he called his disciples. He believed he healed with psychic power and that, like Jesus, he bore the pain of those around him.

From the viewpoint of the world's detractors, this perspective of Elvis as the occultist is generally unnoticed. Again we say with Paul the things of the Spirit are foolishness to those who do not have the Spirit (1 Corinthians 2:14). Thus most do not discern the offence of Elvis' occult involvement. Yet here lay the source of the singer's formidable power. Those who were close tell how he could hypnotise his audiences. Hypnotism, like Rock itself another way to abandon the mind, is of no matter to most people today. At concerts he would read from Blavatsky's book "The Voice of Silence" to indoctrinate his audiences; the book, "Elvis" by Arthur Goldman, tells us that his gospel group "Voice" was named after the book.

Next we come to the Beatles. Who was George Harrison referring to when he wrote of his "Sweet Lord" in "My Sweet Lord", the popular song that captured the hearts of many of the parents? We can know that George wrote the foreword to "Bhagavita-Gita As It Is" an introduction to the Hindu religion available in England, and there no doubt find the answer to our question. Hinduism is the religion at the root of the Blavatsky theosophy which packaged it for the New Age, but unlike Presley the Beatles went to spend time in India. They can be credited with promoting T.M. in the West just as Presley gave us Rock n'Roll. Yet Presley too was a devotee of a Hindu mystic, Paramahansa Yogananda, founder of the Self-Realisation Fellowship;* the Beatles were disciples of the West's merchant of T.M., the Indian Guru, Maharishi Mahesh Yogi.

So much for the musicians; what about the Music? What about Rock n'Roll? Back in 1954 an American disc jockey found the phrase to describe the music, and from the ghetto community he took a descriptive expression used for fornication: rock and roll. Yet the expressive sex in the dance and music representing the evil of the New Morality was again but the thin end of the wedge. The discerning of the world had no difficulty in recognising there was something more subtle and even more serious that went mainly

* "Rock - Practical Help for those who listen to the words and don't like what they hear" by Bob Larson (Tyndale House, Wheaton, Illinois, U.S.A. - 1980).

undiscerned. The Rock beat, long used for calling up spirits by the pagan tribes of the world, was now unknowingly applied on a vast scale in the music of the West. Apart from the message and the lyrics, both significant though mostly not recognised, the evil element peculiar to Rock music is found in the beat. The effect is optimised in conjunction with the strobe lighting and other effects in the Disco, and truly what we have, even though Elvis "the King of Rock and Roll" no longer lives, is a counterfeit worship. Man has turned his worship from the true King. What we see is not the worship of God through Jesus Christ, the King, and who is the Rock. What we have is pagan deceptions hung on Hindu philosophies and based on the worship of false gods seen in the East for thousands of years.

Apart from the beat, music can expose us to another deception. The words can be projected at a level below the conscious awareness, yet the repetition is said to find for it a place in the mind. Thus the normal mental vetting process, admittedly probably very low in many today, is circumvented. Some pop singers have adopted this technique, and without the listener realising it, exhortations to drug-taking or sexual immorality have been heard and retained in the memory. Again some cassettes conceal hidden sounds revealed when the tape is played backwards, and the mind apparently picks up these subliminal messages and translates them.*

Hinduism and Helena Blavatsky's Theosophy is the simple key to understanding New Age philosophy. There followed Theosophist Alice Bailey whose writings describe the New Age. Music was important to them as it is important to God; Lucifer himself was responsible for it until, through his rebellion, he was cast by God upon the Earth (Isaiah 14:12). Lucifer is known as Satan and music is important to him still. Alice Bailey, hearing "The Tibetan" - the name given to her spirit guide - was listening to the same deceptive spirits who speak to Channeling Mediums. Correct though they may have been so far, we cannot trust what they say. Elvis Presley was one who was led through Music, Drugs and the Occult

* "It's Never been So Late Before" by Frederick A. Tatford (Ambassador Productions, Belfast - 1986).

to misplace this trust. Led by Elvis and others, and most important by the music itself, like those following the Pied Piper, the deceived ones today follow pagan ways and the gurus of the East. Indeed from New Age teaching founded on the theosophy of Blavatsky and Bailey, it is quite clear that music is significant in the New Age.*

We shall look at other occultic music too, but here we have taken a brief look at Rock and the evil religion behind it. Satan purposes death, both spiritual and physical and there have been many since Elvis who have found it; many like him, by their own hand. Yet according to their Hindu/Theosophist teaching they don't see before them an eternity separated from God. They expect reincarnation. They don't see Hell awaiting them (Revelation 20:12-15), but rather the counterfeit idea of re-birth, working out their own salvation, their Karma. They seek, according to Hindu/New Age teaching to pay the price themselves. They do not know that Jesus already paid the price of our sin and that He is the only way for their salvation (1 John 2:23).

New Age Music

Rock and Disco quite evidently has its place in stealing from young people the self-control which the Bible warns we should jealously guard. Scenes of young people out of control are all too well known. Yet when "The New Age Catalogue," the "manual for the true conoisseur of the New Age," writes of New Age Music it isn't referring to Rock music. Steven Halpern of Halpern Sounds tells us that although definitions may vary, for the first time since the birth of the blues, jazz and rock, a new genre of music has "manifested on our planet." New Age music, he tells us, reflects our times, and encourages the integration of the inner and outer being, offering "an audio portrait of world peace." He writes of the "healing art of music" and a long-overdue reversal of the trend that limited the role of music. In line with New Age thinking, he sees music, like alternative medicine and all the rest, as spiritual. Correctly he points

* "The Externalisation of the Hierarchy" by Alice Bailey.

to the use of New Age music in meditation, in relaxation, in hospitals and in executive board rooms. Again and again, New Agers point to the benefits of what they are involved with, and they seek to back it up with science.

The search is for a "new consciousness" and Halpern is satisfied that research has proven that music is a "carrier wave for consciousness." He adds that it's not just the music itself but the "vibrational state" of the artist when he is composing or recording to which we respond. The New Age language - language without meaning - is ever present. It is all a matter of describing the energy, the force, the at-oneness, the consciousness, the attunement as they seek to be part of, and at one with, the creation, just as God is supposed to be "a part of" or "at-one-with" his creation.

But the fact remains, and the warning here is important, that "New Age Music" has arrived, and in America the 1987 Music Awards for the first time included the category of New Age Music. It is true, as some are quick to point out, that the New Age is really very old, as old as Babylon in fact. Yet let us not deny the new forms in which it is springing up in our day. In "America - The Sorcerer's New Apprentice - the Rise of New Age Shamanism,"* Dave Hunt writes that this New Age music is already generating 100 million dollars in annual sales, and he adds, "United Airlines was quick to devote an entire channel to New Age Music" for its passengers, and Lincoln-Mercury, BMW and Honda were among the first auto manufacturers to jump on this skyrocketing bandwagon with the use of New Age music for promoting their products. By November 1987 the "Los Angeles Times" could report in its business section that 'radio stations that play New Age music exclusively have suddenly sprung up in virtually every major U.S. city.' Much of this music is designed to help induce the altered state of consciousness that is essential to New Age spirituality, but seldom are purchasers advised of this fact."

I can understand that the merchants of this music firmly believe that a wearied generation has a need of this music. They know it will help with relaxation and give people a

* published by Harvest House (Eugene Oregon, 1988).

better feeling. They know not the dangers and it wouldn't occur to them that any warning was needed. It seldom occurs to a Christian evangelist, when he is preaching the Gospel, to warn that coming to Jesus Christ involves much, means giving up much, and means a changed life; of course, he is *certain* that Christ is the answer. New Age promoters are also *certain*. They promote their wares with the conviction that follows from that, and thus they succeed. They don't know they have a powerful devil on their side, and that so far as God allows, he may masquerade as an angel of light. In few places is there better evidence of this than with New Age music. As a New Ager I heard it. I heard what the airline passengers are now hearing. It *is* very soothing indeed.

The world is more and more aware of what is happening and the following report of a ''Global Rock Festival'' in the Peter Simple column of the ''Daily Telegraph'' put it this way:

The Global Rock Festival is itself a symbol of the collapse of European civilisation and of the collapse of the Christian religion. It also offers a glimpse, perhaps the most horrendous so far, of the possible future of the human race if the dream of ''One World'' should ever be realised.

In that nightmare world all the arts of all the human civilisations, all the customs, all the traditions, all the religions would be petrified in museums, superseded by satellite-borne ''information-systems'', filling the air with international musical uproar, with messages and images of humane inhumanity concerning ''the arts'', scientific marvels in ''space'', population control, health and hygiene, the duty of all to be equal irrespective of sex, race or anything else you can think of.

Fortunately, however horrible the events which will avert it, that dream will never be realised. 18th July 1985.

As so often happens our commentators get the analysis right, and then reach the wrong conclusion!

Eastern Religions, Witchcraft and Paganism

The signs of the times are reflected in the moves we see towards a one-world religion. I believe we should not mistake the particular significance of the 1986 gathering of the world's religious leaders at Assisi brought together by the Pope.* These included the Eastern Religions from which the New Age has sprung. There were witches and pagans, certainly no more decadent than Rome itself, but African snake worshippers and Red Indian medicine men would have been unheard of in such a gathering just a few years ago.

In the West we increasingly have multi-religious societies. Witchcraft and paganism, quite apart from the so-called white witchcraft of holistic health and the seance room, is increasing too. Most of the world is pagan; the United Nations represents it throughout its activity. East has needed to meet West. The introduction has been made. The Imam Mahdi, the Fifth Budda and all the rest have long since been awaited in the East. Now in the West the New Agers await the Christ. Meanwhile, not surprisingly, the leadership is in the West. Efforts are centred on the New Age movement and in Rome, which we deal with later.

Ecology and Population: What are the Facts?

Christians are properly concerned with many of the questions which occupy ecologists. The New Age pervades in this area too.

Ecology, the study of the interaction of persons with their environment, broadly involves the natural resources and amenities available for the population that needs to draw upon them. In the scheme of one-world government, population control will be an important consideration. It is certain that there is a problem with the growth of world population, yet

* There was a separate gathering at Assisi in 1986. This one was sponsored by the World Wild Life Fund, and both were significant events on the New Age scene.

91

it seems to be by no means certain that it is in the interests of the global planners to focus on the provision *for* the population. In "Globalism: America's Demise,"** by William M. Bowen, Jnr, we can read that Global government must control the *people,* and that "population roll back" i.e to *reduce* the *world population* to a *controllable* number would be practical. A likely purpose is *not* just to get the population numbers in line with natural resources. Rather the reports seem to suggest that enormous natural resources are being concealed. We deal with this question in "Understanding the New Age - World Government and World Religion."

The United Nations, also examined in that book, is concerned about population; it is very much more than a forum for the world's political leaders to gather. It proliferates agencies able to serve as the civil service departments of a one-world government. In 1969 the Executive Director of the United Nations Fund for Population Activities (UNFPA) had little more than an office and a great deal of enthusiasm. That is what the British Minister of Overseas Development wrote in the preface of a book written by the Executive Director some ten years later. The book was a four hundred and fifty-six page look at the concepts and policies which had guided UNFPA in those first ten years. Five years later, and introducing the Executive Director's next book "Reflections on Population" in the Foreword, the Secretary-General of the U.N., Javier Perez de Cuellar wrote:

"One of the most urgent of these global problems is population. By the year 2000, the global population is expected to reach 6.1 billion. The awesome reality of this number of people who will inhabit our earth in the relatively near future has a direct bearing on virtually every political, economic and social issue now confronting us... the problem remains enormous and unavoidable. It is without doubt one of the most difficult issues that Member States and the United Nations have to deal with on a national and international

** Published by Huntington House, Inc. (USA) - 1984.

basis. Religious, ideological and cultural values are involved as well as intensely personal and human considerations.''

Religious, ideological and cultural values as well as "intensely personal" and human considerations; does this involve anything more than birth control and population relocation? In the words of "The Global 2000 Report to the President", an era of "unprecedented global co-operation and commitment is essential." What are the solutions that the planners have in mind?

We have seen answers to that question given in chapter four by Barbara Marx Hubbard, John Randolph Price, and the Spirit Guide, Asher. Their message about cleansing will be heard in the New Age movement.

New Age in Business

I was reflecting that I had spent half of a working lifetime in the world of business, and a few years writing about the New Age, and yet I knew little about the New Age in Business.

Then a copy of the New York "International Herald Tribune" (3rd. October 1986) came my way. This is an area where the New Age is relatively new and fast gaining ground. Since that time there has been no shortage of evidence. In the New York paper I read that representatives of some of America's largest corporations, including I.B.M., A.T. & T. and General Motors met in New Mexico to discuss how metaphysics, the occult and Hindu mysticism might help executives compete in the world marketplace. Then I saw that at Stanford University's well regarded Graduate School of Business, the syllabus for a seminar on "Creativity in Business" included meditation, chanting, "dream work", the use of Tarot cards and discussion of the "New Age Capitalist."

A common view among New Age thinkers is that major corporations should be looked at "holistically", not with the pyramid-style organisational responsibility, but with power

* Published by Pergamon Press - 1985.

shared among all employees. Over here in Britain, in the words of the Findhorn Foundation's promotion handout for their conference "From Organisation to Organism," viewing the organisation as organism within a social, cultural and ecological context is providing a new framework within which individuals and groups can experiment with new forms. The handout describes the changing business scene: Large organisations are refining their structures to create smaller, more responsive units; cooperative ventures of all sizes are on the increase to make the wisest use of available resources; new methods to unleash the full creative potential of the individual are in the forefront of a newly renamed arm of the organisation... human resources management. Words such as intuition, enabling, flow state, alignment, self-actualisation and stress management are now becoming commonplace in the vocabulary of managers and business people.

The magazine "California Business" reported (1986) that its study of 500 company owners and presidents had found that more than half said they had resorted to some form of "consciousness-raising" technique.

The Business Scene in Britain

As soon as I opened my file on "New Age in Business" in 1986 it began to fill up.

The profile of one astrologer was given to us in a half page of a national newspaper.* This lady had been working in business and commerce for 40 years and now advised 48 companies about expansion plans, appointments, and the suitability of people for board membership. She reminds us of the situation in Europe and points out that for a long time astrology has been used in business in France, Germany and Switzerland. "Every business has a life of its own and this is reflected internally. Just like a person, a company is a blueprint of the time and place in which it was born and I can tell you how it will behave or perform in the future. The movement of the planets are the ebb and flow of energy.

* Daily Telegraph "Wednesday Matters" by Jenny Rees 31 December 1986.

Business life has rhythms, just like the life of an individual.''
So says this business consultant.

In the same article it was natural for the reporter to seek an academic and professional opinion. Peter Makin, occupational psychologist in the Department of Management Science at Manchester University's Institute of Science and Technology, tells us "You may not get the right man for the right job using this technique, but you may well prevent the wrong man from being given the wrong job... Plenty of work has been done on the statistical tendency of certain birthsigns found in certain professions. You may well get someone applying for a job with a personality that makes him more suitable for another.''

It is interesting that in a survey only one out of 108 questionnaires returned to Makin admitted the use of astrology. The same survey showed eight per cent reporting the use of handwriting analysis. This also highlighted the strengths and weaknesses of an individual personality and character, we were told.

Alternative Medicine

Whilst AID is surely posing the most terrible threat to the health of mankind, the area of health CARE which assuredly poses the greatest threat is Alternative Medicine.

What we have is an enormous range of therapies, alternatives to medical science, which are finding an ever increasing number of willing patients. This is the more remarkable because only a few years ago many of the practitioners would not be accepted as having any valid scientific basis.

One General Practitioner described the procedure of one of the testing techniques used: The idea was to identify dietary substances that would be harmful to the patient. Small amounts of the substance under test were in turn placed upon the subject's tongue whilst the practitioner attempted to lower the subject's arm as it was held extended first above the head, then about waist level, and then lower. Apparently it was quite easy for the subject to resist these attempts to move his arm, except when any dietary substance 'harmful' to him was placed upon his tongue when he seemed powerless to resist the force applied by the practitioner. Then a similar procedure was repeated, but this time instead of the substance being placed on the tongue they remained in their unopened bottle and the bottle was placed on the skin of the abdomen. This had the same apparent effect on muscle power, and the harmful substances thus identified were the same in both instances - fish, tea, sugar and monosodium glutamate*.

Whatever scientific basis there may be for this, it illustrates the unconventionality of the Holistic Health movement. What we have is an enormous A to Z range from Acupuncture through to the therapies based on Zen and other meditation techniques. They can mostly be shown to be patently ridiculous. Yet the problem is much more serious than that would suggest. Alternative Medicine incorporates within it a great number of occult practices, in themselves significant in the New Age.

New Agers focus on the creation rather than on the Creator and in so doing they discover the mysterious hidden secrets of the creation. They are also earnest in their desires to protect the creation. In shorthand language, focus is evidenced on one hand by the occult involvement of New Agers, and on the other by their interest in nature.

The focus on nature leads many to Earth Worship. These two elements (Discovering the secrets of the creation where the Bible forbids enquiry and protecting the creation) reflected in the New Age movement itself are also found in Alternative Medicine. For example Psychic Healing and Radiesthesia (divination, for example with the pendulum) involve forbidden discovery, a direct and very dangerous encounter with the spirit realm, whereas Homoeopathy and a careless use of herbal remedies, in addition to that, can involve a wrong focus on nature.

Secondly, Alternative Medicine is appropriately looked at as a signpost for the New Age because these therapies are launching points for those who will go deeper into deception. The dangerous deception is SPIRITUAL deception. As man

* "Understanding Alternative Medicine" by Roy Livesey (New Wine Press, 1988).

focusses upon himself, not particularly looking after his health but seeking his healing in whatever place he can find it, except he exercises care and has discernment, he will find himself where Satan and spirits masquerade as angels of light (2 Corinthians 11:14) but where those to whom the things of the Spirit are foolishness (1 Corinthians 2:14) will not fear to tread.

The spiritual battle is real in Alternative Medicine as Satan and his demon spirits purpose to keep men dead spiritually until they are dead physically and thus without hope of the salvation promised to those who turn to Jesus Christ. How easy it seems to be for Satan to keep the focus, often of Christian and non-Christian alike, on physical existence and the capacity for enjoyment of the world's pleasures (2 Timothy 3:4)! This gives rise to the first question heard for any alternative therapy: "Does it work?"

We see throughout our review of the strange New Age innovations of our day, that this question all are asking, or the aspects that most are aware of, miss the more subtle deceptions at work. We shall see too that where spiritual matters of the New Age are concerned there is little advantage on the side of those with the benefits of a high level of education. We can be grateful in a measure for the report of the British Medical Association on Alternative Medicine*. They gave a general "thumbs down". They could find precious little science. Indeed there is precious little to find. They were asking the question: "Does it work?" Indeed Alternative Medicine most certainly DOES work. It works in very many cases, but more seriously, OCCULT Alternative Medicine (which is most of it) can have a serious effect in EVERY case. There is a price to pay for involvement, however innocently, in the occult spiritual realm. The price has to be paid for those counterfeit miracles of occult healing, and they do happen often. It is healing that science and the ways of the doctor are unable to explain.

* "Alternative Therapy" (British Medical Association, 1986).

Pray for the Royal Family

The Royal Family has long been prey for these occult deceptions. Homoeopathy is the therapy where, prompted by Royal support of it, a large faculty of qualified medical doctors have been practising for many generations. Prince Charles is just one among the Royal Family who has endorsed Alternative Medicine as a whole, but Royal involvement with the paranormal runs much deeper.

"The Prince and the Paranormal"** by John Dale is an important book, the result of careful research into the occult and spiritual interests of the Prince of Wales and the Royal Family going back several generations. As Christians we are to pray for our rulers and Dale's book not only gives us an excellent summary and insight into one family's involvement in the New Age, but it provides a direction and perhaps an urgency for our prayers.

In Dale's words, was Homoeopathy and Alternative Medicine "The Royal Key"? Certainly for many, Alternative Medicine is an entry point to the dangerous world of the New Age and the occult.

We do as Christians need to pray for the Royal Family, remembering that the Queen in particular *does* have an important ruling role. It simply is not true that she does not, and, whatever modern conventions might be, each Act of Parliament *must* be signed by the sovereign, and this is *her* approval. The Bible says:

"I exhort therefore, that, first of all, supplications, prayers, intercessions, and giving thanks, be made for all men; For kings, and for all that are in authority, that we may lead a quiet and peaceable life in all godliness and honesty" (1 Timothy 2:1-2).

"The Prince and the Paranormal" by John Dale is probably the first detailed study of Prince Charles and the Royal Family's beliefs in psychic and spiritual phenomena, and whilst not presented from a Chrisitan perspective, I believe it has all the marks of good accurate reporting on

** - available from Bury House Christian Books, Clows Top, Kidderminster, Worcs. DY14 9HX where a large supply of this out-of-print book is held.

a vast range of occult Royal involvement. As such it is recommended not only for the useful description of New Age activity that is presented but also to show where prayer is needed.

Holograms and Images - Interesting Opportunities in The New Age

I attended an exhibition of holograms, seemingly significant in the New Age. The hologram is a three-dimensional projection made with the interaction of laser beams and the significance in the New Age, according to George Leonard in "The Silent Pulse"*, seems to connect with the Hindu idea of the "Net of Jewels", in which every jewel, every piece of the universe, contains every other piece. In our look at Hinduism we have noted the idea that "all-is-one" is central to that all-embracing religion. Leonard sees this as the core of all mysticism. At the exhibition I learned that an entire hologram, in picture form, bought for a few pounds, could be smashed to produce that same complete picture in each of its parts.

David Pond, writing in "The New Age Catalogue"* about systems of divination, tells us his New Age perspective. Each piece of the holographic image contains the same information as the whole picture, and applied to consciousness, the analogy implies that each individual contains the information of the "collective consciousness" within himself. "Divination creates a vehicle for accessing this information. Each person can be both a receiver and a transmitter of universal knowledge. In the art of divination you seek to align yourself with the clearest channel of information between your essential nature and the wisdom inherent in the universe." Thus, what we have, and what we saw at the exhibition of holograms, was the application of science to support occult philosophy.

The philosophy is the philosophy of unity, or in Hinduistic

---

* published by Bantam Books, New York (1981).

* published by Doubleday - 1988.

terms, all-is-one; we are all at-one with the creation and the Creator. The philosophy is not the Christian message of the atonement for sin, made possible by the atoning blood of Jesus Christ. The philosophy is, a corruption of that wonderful atonement, the New Age at-one-ment. The philosophy is *"after the tradition of men, after the rudiments of the world, and not after Christ"* (Colossians 2:8).

Appropriately, and in line with the at-one-ment, the ecumenism and the syncretism of our day, in order to enter the exhibition, which was presented by "Christian Aid" in support of its Africa Appeal, I was given a lapel sticker. It was triangular, and at the centre was the "all-seeing-eye", the symbol of Osiris from the Egyptian trinity. The location of the exhibition was Southwark Cathedral in London. In that borough there are two cathedrals, and mistakenly I went first to Southwark Roman Catholic Cathedral and was told: "No, I think you will find the exhibition in Southwark Church of England Cathedral." It was there I found the hologram exhibition.

I don't suppose for one moment that the Dean and Chapter of Southwark had registered any philosophical connection as they agreed to stage such an exhibition in the cathedral. However discernment is quite a different matter from taking hold of events, as I have myself mistakenly done, slotting them into a politico-conspiratorial scenario. One wrong impression I had to correct concerned another cathedral, this time in New York. I found the story of the laser equipment so extraordinarily fascinating that I even related it in some detail in one of my regular circular mailings. In July 1984 I wrote:

'Constance Cumbey in her book "The Hidden Dangers of the Rainbow" (1983) tells us David Spangler, a New Age leader, said in a meeting in Southfield, Michigan, 1st February 1982, that laser beam projectors had been installed on the top of St. John the Divine, the Episcopal cathedral in New York City. Spangler, who has said that Luciferic initiation will be required to enter the New Age, has his sermons featured in the cathedral. Cumbey writes: "I talked to lighting experts to see what laser beams projectors are

capable of and I was told they can be beamed onto tele-communications satellites.

The New Agers have several of these at their disposal. When the lasers bounce from the satellite back to earth, the light rays can be bent in such a manner as to appear that flames are coming from the sky. These satellites can also be used to project a three-dimensional holographic image viewed by up to one third of the earth's population.

There is even technology to make the image speak in the language of the areas to which it is beamed... Christians should remember that the motive behind the New Age Movement is Lucifer's desire to be worshipped as God.'''

Much factual evidence is contained there, and we *do* need to heed carefully the purposes of Satan according to Scripture. Lucifer *does* desire to be worshipped as god and that is Satan's purpose. It is certainly happening now, knowingly and unknowingly, in numerous groups, freemasonry among them. However, interesting and definitely-New-Age though the equipment on the cathedral may have been, if we are not careful the evil one is able to take the Christian's focus from the truth of God's word. Also on a factual point, one usually reliable Christian source has now reported that the lasers were rented and have since been returned! Satan works in mystery and they are mysteries that have to be discerned.

Yet let us understand the philosophy of the hologram. Every part of the whole demands absorption of the part into the whole. Every aspect of life and every separate community are to be integrated in the whole. That is the direction where the New Age leads. Like the drop in the ocean, our identity is supposed to be lost as we become at one with all about us. Otherwise, as "Asher" might tell us, we have no business being here!

101

7

The Cults - Drifting Towards the New Age

"Who, me in a cult? That could never happen to me." Are we going to say that many in cults today, including many of their leaders, didn't start off as professing Christian believers? However broadly or narrowly we define what is a cult, we may not be very far off from the place where we end, once we allow doctrine that departs *at all* from the Word of God written in the Bible and revealed to us by the Holy Spirit.

There is no great merit in providing a careful definition of a cult, even if that were possible. Also the doctrines of most of the major cults have appeared in what seem endless numbers of books listing and analysing one cult after another: Jehovah's Witnesses, Christian Science, Mormons, Seventh Day Adventism, the Unity School of Christianity, and so on. The list can be enormous.

Another way to look at the cults is to consider them all - hundreds of them - within a range. At the one end we can set those with seemingly little basis at all in Scripture; at the other will be those which, to all but the discerning Bible-believing Christian, might seem identical with Christianity. The word "cult" is one the enemy can use to conceal what is going on in a complex collection of counterfeits. It is also a term ecumenists can use to describe Bible-believing Christians! Then cult is a term which Christians can use, often in a not very helpful way, to describe a movement where serious error is to be found. "Cult" is however a useful description of warning that can cause Christians to look more closely and ask: *Where* does it not measure up to Scripture?

A Way to Godhood?

Like the Eastern religions on which many of them are founded, the cults are based upon the lie which is at the root and basis of all Satan's deceptions. Genesis 3:4-5 says that Eve would not surely die and that when she ate the fruit her eyes would be opened to know good and evil. Cults do not usually see Man as separate from his Creator.

Satan is bringing the counterfeit experiences that encourage our aspirations to godhood. I was talking to a young school-leaver, and his relaxation had consisted of leaving his body for a couple of hours to sit in a hay field. He said he "really needed" that two-hours of "relaxation"; it was *really* meditation. It was meditation which involved switching off the mind and relinquishing control, not the true meditation which must be on the Word of God. The experience was very *real* to him. That was his *reality*. Apart from feeling the need, he felt special. Some reach the state of oneness with the universe travelling out-of-body to other planets. A medium I once consulted pointed to the vase on the shelf and informed me she felt at one with it. Is it surprising that such experiences lead to aspirations of godhood?

At the one end of our range of cults it is clear many have aspired to godhood and would openly say so. At the opposite end nothing could be further from the imagination of the cultist. He might even consider himself a Bible-believing Christian. Yet the effect can be that we bring such a focus on ourselves that we do become as gods. All of the occult philosophy is united in believing that the real self of man is God. We battle not against flesh and blood but against the powers of darkness, (Ephesians 6:12) and the range of cults these days is extending to infiltrate Christian fellowships.

Cults encourage, each in their own way, the development of what Man can do for himself. That is a very easy place for Satan to begin, and it suits his purpose when Man focusses not on Jesus Christ but on self. It is the way of Man to justify himself. *"Every way of a man is right in his own eyes: but the Lord pondereth the hearts"* (Proverbs 21:2). It is the way of unredeemed man to try and prove himself, and indeed to save himself. Yet there is no man that has power over the

Spirit (Ecclesiastes 8:8), nor can he *"by any means redeem his brother, nor give to God a ransom for him"* (Psalm 49:7). It is the way of unredeemed man to seek the approval of his leaders, to seek the approval of his church and the congratulation of those around him. It is the way of men to aspire to something they can comprehend and to what their leaders can identify with. It is the way of Man to travel these roads, apart from what the Bible says, until he is born again. Satan, with the cults that he has founded, meets us wherever we are, unceasing and tireless in his efforts. As believers we are never home until we reach the end of the road. We *could* find ourselves in a cult. The New Testament was written to the Church. Peter wrote *"Be sober, be vigilant; because your adversary the devil, as a roaring lion, walketh about, seeking whom he may devour"* (1 Peter 5:8). I do not believe any of us dare say, "It could never happen to me." Rather let us hold fast to the truth of God's word and see that, apart from Him, *it could*.

"Secret Cult": School of Economic Science (S.E.S.)

An enormous amount of information about cult activities has come from the United States, the launching ground for so many cults founded on the ideas of human potential and Eastern religion. Here my purpose is to look briefly at three cults flourishing in Britain. The three are each of a different kind. At the extreme end of our range there is the School of Economic Science (S.E.S.). In the words of its Prinicpal in a letter to the London "Standard" the school has the aim "to study and teach the natural laws governing relations between men in society." The letter went on, "From the early consideration of these laws in the realm of economics, students began to ask deeper questions about the fundamentals of man's existence itself. This step into philosophy, which is the love of wisdom, was most natural."

In 1984 two "Standard" journalists published what it described as "a full exposé of a strange and destructive organisation that is penetrating the corridors of power". They called their book "Secret Cult", and in it there was quoted another letter to 'The Standard'. This presented an example of the understanding of Sanskrit and of the Hindu perspective of another senior man involved with S.E.S.:

Much has been made during the interviews of our use of Sanskrit, and naturally, many prospective parents are puzzled and perhaps a little sceptical about this. The young children begin with writing and sounding the characters which have the advantage of being wholly phonetic. They move on to simple words expressing concepts which have no precise English equivalent. But let me emphasise that the point in no way is to turn the children into Hindus. The point of the exercise is to help them discover more about themselves and the natural working of all their faculties. In any case, this elementary study of Sanskrit is a great help when other languages are introduced later on. The philosophical teaching they receive derives principally from conversations between... the founder of the School itself, and the Shankaracharya whom he meets every couple of years in India. These conversations are characterised by their great simplicity and relevance to the questions and problems of the modern world. By tradition the Shankaracharyas have been ready to answer the questions of all who have come to seek their guidance, whether of their own tradition or of another.

The essence of this philosophy is the essential unity which pervades everything and is itself a characteristic of the omniscient and omnipotent Creator from whom everything flows. None of this is in conflict with the principal tenets of the great religions, and it is certainly our wish that a child coming from a religious home, be it Christian, Jewish, Muslim or Hindu, should gain a deeper penetration of the essential truths of their own religion and their own tradition. *

The two "Standard" journalists, for their own reasons not wanting to expound their views on Hindu philosophy in this context, give a useful introduction to the Shankaracharya:

Two notes of caution must be held firmly in mind. Firstly, criticism of the SES is not intended as a criticism of Hindu philosophy. It is the way that philosophy is applied which

* ''Secret Cult'' by Peter Hounam and Andrew Hogg (Lion Publishing, Tring, Herts. 1984).

prompts our concern about the British-based cult... *
Christians can be grateful to Hounam and Hogg for their
exposé. Let us be clear however that the great danger *is* in
the Hindu philosophy and in the Sanskrit language.

In cults there is a hierarchy. For example, in Freemasonry
the Duke of Kent is seen to be the man at the top, but there
are thirty higher degrees where are found the more powerful
yet less well-known. In the S.E.S. it is clear that a significant
personality is the Shankaracharya. He is looked to as I looked
to my guru. There are many in India in possession of what
is called "the ancient knowledge." It is clear from the letter
that Sanskrit is believed to have much to commend it and
that it is not recognised for the evil that it is. The truth is
that Sanskrit is the ancient and sacred language of the Hindus
in India. It was (and is) the language devoted to the deities
of India. The Vedas are the ancient scriptures of India. Veda
is a Sanskrit word derived from "vid" which means "to
know", and the Vedas comprise the ancient knowledge and
wisdom transmitted by the enlightened ones, the Brahmin
caste, through the ages in the form of poems, hymns, charms,
incantations, chants, mantras and so forth. Here we have the
fruit of the tree of knowledge of Genesis 3:5, the alternative
and counterfeit of Jesus Christ, the Word, who is life.

It seems clear that on the part of the writer there may be
no *intention* to turn the children to Hinduism, the religion
that accomodates all but the Bible-believing Christian. I can
understand his position as he expresses it. I was a Hindu,
and I didn't realise it! I was a New Ager and didn't realise it!

It is a main thesis of this book that Hinduism is the relgion
that accomodates many others. It is the religion bringing men,
whatever their faith, into the New Age. The Bible calls us
to spiritual warfare and to battle for the truth that brings
freedom. That is a battle not against flesh and blood but
against the demonic forces (Ephesians 6:12).

God knows of Satan's wiles. He knows how Satan seeks
to make life very complicated and encourage our desire to
go to "wiser" men for help. He must have seen it as
inevitable in these troubled and materialistic times that

* "Secret Cult" (Lion Publishing).

Western Man would have an envy for those with the "peace" and knowledge of the East. Because God knew these things He gave us His Word by which to live. It is the Word which brings a real peace, and the Truth which sets men free.

Buchmanism, The Oxford Group, Moral Re-Armament (MRA)

Another significant movement which is relatively little known is Moral Re-Armament (MRA) formerly known as the Oxford Group. This cult or movement, founded by Frank Buchman, is somewhere in the middle of the range we have envisaged. Its origins are not to be found in the Eastern religions. Rather we have a nominally Christian group which has drifted in that direction through failure to focus on Jesus Christ, and through its openness to other religions. I heard one Bible teacher speak of the devil. 'If you open the door a *little* way then just like your dog, he will be able to squeeze in.' Moral Re-Armament left the door open when they resolved to focus not on Jesus Christ, but on what they call the "four absolutes" - honesty, purity, unselfishness and love.

As a university student my interest in politics was able to blossom and I became the chairman of my political party in the Student Union. At the same time I was the student chairman of the United Nations group. Through my position in these groups, a target for the attention of Moral Re-Armament, I became attracted to the teaching of MRA. It made sense to focus on the four absolutes. For the next twenty years I tried, in my own strength, to live by those standards. Without knowing Jesus Christ and acknowledging Him as Saviour and Lord I was bound to fail, and I did.

I believe my eyes were taken further from Jesus Christ through focus on these standards. It was a focus on self, a self-righteous attempt at the impossible. I was no longer part of an MRA group after leaving the university, and then twenty years later the flame was rekindled through what *seemed* to be a God-ordained meeting with MRA people. It seemed then that a continuing fellowship and support with MRA people would be the answer. I threw my heart into

MRA in a new way. I attended their conferences and I made special friends with a Hindu. Shortly after joining up with MRA again I became a "searcher" in the occult realm. The Hindu ways and the yoga made so much sense to me. I was finding the peace which I had sought. I didn't know it was a counterfeit peace. I couldn't possibly know it wasn't that peace that comes from knowing the Lord Jesus Christ, that peace which passes all understanding. At the climax of a traumatic and harrowing time from the effects of my occult involvement, I was quick to renounce all that I recognised as occult. On becoming a Christian, I renounced and repented of all the occult involvement as I remembered it. However, even after several months growing fast in the Lord, I could see nothing but good in MRA.

One of the books I read was "Hidden Warfare" by David Watson. I was, I believed, very "teachable", and it was unlikely I would at that stage in my Christian walk be very quick to question anything that David Watson had to say. Then I came to a reference about MRA. I read that Moral Re-Armament was a cult. "Who me in a cult? That could never happen to me." I couldn't and wouldn't believe it. I had been *in* it; I should know! I hadn't yet learned what I now know; you never ask anyone who is into the occult or who is a member of a cult and expect to get the right answers. I was still involved with MRA. *My* views were not in the least relevant. I wrote to David Watson. He replied and I still couldn't see it! This was the spiritual realm. A battle was going on in that dimension. It was not a matter of intellect. Then at last I did hear the Lord, through David Watson's letter. Suddenly I could see it as clear as crystal. I could renounce it and be set free.

The Religious Society of Friends (Quakers)

Freedom and peace are favourite foundations upon which the enemy can build. It's the *truth* that sets men free, but it is *not* easy to speak out against the freedom that Man seeks. Jesus Christ gives us that peace that passes all understanding;

it is *not* easy to convey to the world that the peace *it* seeks to bring is something quite different.

My wife and I visited Molesworth in the time before the American "Cruise" missiles were removed from there. It would have been easy to identify sympathetically with the silent protesters sleeping rough under their tarpaulins. There was a single poster: a large rainbow with the words "Sizewell to Molesworth - Make the Link; break the chain." Here again was that New Age rainbow we have seen many times. Parked alongside the many sleeping campers was the Quaker "command post". Who are the Quakers? I knew they had the official name, "Religious Society of Friends". I knew they were a peaceful organisation. Nowhere had I ever heard anything spoken against Quaker ideas. I thought they were at least a nominally Christian denomination, but seeing them at this centre of inter-faith witness and worship (there was an inter-faith chapel) I decided to find out more. From amongst all the many volumes on the cults that I had seen there was nothing. Indeed but for David Watson's "Hidden Warfare" and my own previous writings there is to my knowledge nothing published from a Christian source identifying MRA as a cult or religious movement. The Society of Friends (the Quakers) is similar. Apart from the Quaker's own literature I found only a single duplicated tract.

Barry Napier of the Christian Research Institute* wrote the tract on the basis only of what the Quakers say about themselves in their own writings. He begins by reminding us that Quakers are known worldwide for their good works but they are certainly not Christian; Quakerism is a peculiar humanistic religion which accepts other religions as true. "The Society of Friends has always resisted the codifying of its faith in creeds and dogma; it is not easy to present a sharply drawn statement (of belief)." What a difference from the Bible! Another Quaker writer tells us: "Quakers discover God in and through their relationships with others" ... but is the god they speak of the God of the Bible? Rather than accepting Jesus Christ as Saviour, they find God themselves by being loving to others - hence their peacefulness, their

* P.O. Box 415, Sketty, Swansea SA2 9AZ. U.K.

efforts for peace and their good works generally. Rather than seeing God as a personal Creator He is an 'inner reality.'

A Quaker experience of God is "to be still" with others. "Let us give the name 'Silence' to what others prefer to call 'The Word'." A great deal of spiritual power is attached to this kind of silent meeting where it is claimed that the "spirit" will visit people and order their lives.

Still drawing from the Quakers' own writings we see they are "anxious to seek the truth wherever it may lead them," but that always they "start this search within their own experience, discovering truth individually and corporately ... being tolerant of the convictions of others." They admit "other Christian groups find us highly unsatisfactory," and this follows from the willingness in the Society of Friends to give status to the Book of Mormon, the Koran or any other philosophical and religious teaching. Members are encouraged to "read the Bible and other writings which reveal the ways of God." They don't see that the only way to God is through Jesus Christ; members are encouraged to "receive fresh light from whatever quarter it may come." "Whatever quarter" even includes ideas which oppose Christianity. The aim of a Quaker meeting is not to meet with God, but to "have a sense of communion with others, sympathy and understanding." The world will rarely object to the ways of the Quaker, sincere and self-sacrificing for the needs of others, but what light can they get from one another?

Quakerism is a complex set of philosophical and pseudo-religious beliefs. It is like a Western version of Hinduism. Like Hinduism it accomodates the other systems and views - *except Biblical Christianity.* So, 'good' as Quakerism appears to be, really it is just another deception.

We can see what the School of Economic Science (S.E.S.), Moral Re-Armament (MRA) and the Society of Friends (the Quakers) have in common. They are open to the teachings of other religions and, like the Hindus, they accomodate them. The difficulty for them comes with the biblical Christian who knows the only way to God is through His only Son who came to live as a man, die and pay the penalty for our sins.

The Unification Church (The Moonies)

In Britain, except where we might know of someone who lost a daughter to the cult, or at least read of such a thing in a newspaper, the Moonies have not rated much attention. In America the situation is quite different, and it is for this reason, and because we need to keep an eye on what is happening in America and the deceptions that come from there, we include this section.

We may have met polite Moonie girls on the street selling flowers, or we may have heard of Rev. Moon's jail sentence in the United States for tax evasion, perjury and conspiracy. Yet it would be a great mistake to misunderstand the Moonies; they are on the same course with similar goals to the Christian Kingdom-builders. Moon knows that but of course most Christian Kingdom-builders don't! They aim "to purge the corrupted politicians" so "the sons of god may rule the world under a unified faith." They run subsided low-cost indoctrination courses, with travel and luxury accomodation in Korea, for Christian clergy. Big sums of Moonie money also reach the Presidential election scene; yet of greater interest perhaps is the Moonie Japanese money for Christian ministries in America.

In America in 1988 I found no shortage of information regarding Moonie infiltration into the so-called Christian right to supplement the full-page "Charlotte Observer" article I had seen reproduced in "Christian News" in January. I read there that Moon believed he inherited Jesus Christ's mission "to purge the corrupted politicians" so "the sons of God (may) rule the world" under a united faith. Thus it is an agenda not unlike the builders of the kingdom on earth found on the Christian right in America. There are common goals, and so yoking with Moon is considered by some to be acceptable. Apart from the widespread yoking with Rome seen today, here we have one of the most blatant examples contrary to the words spoken by Paul that we are not to be yoked with unbelievers (2 Corinthians 6:14).

Some events are just not reported very extensively in Britain and I was able to catch up on the background of the Moon infiltration about which I had reported in various issues of "New Age Bulletin" in 1988. To my amazement I came upon a cutting from "Rocky Mountain News" dated 21st August 1985, the day following Moon's release from imprisonment for tax evasion. The occasion was a dinner given in his honour for more than 1,600 religious leaders "within hours" of his release. It was all arranged! Sponsoring the event was the National Committee for God and Freedom whose members include the well-known Christian leader, Jerry Falwell.

Moon told the dinner audience, "I was not there because of my personal actions, yet I did not brood with resentment or hatred for those who persecuted me... Rather I dedicated my time to prayer and meditaiton, for understanding what America must do to fulfill God's will." Falwell said at a news conference earlier in the day, "I think the President should pardon Reverend Moon... I think he was the victim of a railroad job, and I think we all in the religious community are losers because of it." The Bible says:. *"He that saith unto the wicked, Thou art righteous; him shall the people curse, nations shall abhor him"* (Proverbs 24:24). A year or two ago, who could have imagined such fellowship with the leader of the "Moonies" and now, "The Rocky Mountain News" report tells us, Moon won a standing ovation from an audience which punctuated his speech with calls of "Yes!" and "Amen!"

As Christians we need to keep an eye not only on the cults that proliferate in the United States and find their way to Britain. We need to keep careful watch also on the message that Christians bring from that country.

The Christian World View of Business - The Coalition on Revival's Deceptive Perspective

The main evangelical vehicle in the United States for imposing Christian rule on society, and following historical Roman Catholic thinking, is the Coalition on Revival (COR). The doctrine follows broadly along the lines of Christian Reconstruction, Restoration, Kingdom-Now, Dominion Theology, as well as finding common ground with "Reverend" Moon's objectives for improving America.

I have studied two important COR documents. One is "The Christian World View of Business and Occupations", the other is "The Christian World View of Medicine". Because of the particular interest in Medicine, this was the first one examined. The document included 53 "affirmations and denials" over the whole range of medicine and health. Except where I had difficulty with my own understanding, I can say that all 53 sections looked sound and very well thought through with supporting Scripture verses.

Major subjects like AIDS were not ducked: "We affirm that AIDS should be quarantined in a manner similar to other communicable diseases like tuberculosis and typhoid fever." This view following Leviticus 13:46, applied during the Black Death to bring leprosy under control, is not apparently shared by Dr. Mann, the Director of the AIDs programme at the W.H.O (27th January 1988 - "Daily Telegraph"): "There is no public health rationale to justify isolation, quarantine, or other discriminatory measures based solely on a person's HIV infection status or practice of risk behaviours." Dr. Mann may well be right. Yet we may well be guided by the Christian doctors and others who were responsible for the COR Christian World View document. It is a very helpful, and I would say sound, document. So why should we be troubled by the Coalition on Revival with its seventeen Christian World View documents?

"Business and Occupations" is a very different subject from "Medicine" and in this document the deception at the heart of the COR idea was clearly reflected. The COR idea is contained in the Manifesto signed 4th July 1986. This tells us that all Bible-believing Christians "must take a non-neutral stance in opposing, praying against, and speaking against social and moral evils." They list "Atheism ... and evolutionism taught as a monopoly viewpoint in public schools" and "Communism/Marxism, fascism, Nazism and the one-world government of the New Age Movement."

That sounds fine, but what is the ultimate goal? Is it right? The "Business and Occupations" document is concluded with a committment, and place for a signature, to thirteen "Specific Actions" as follows: "... we commit ourselves to the following specific actions, which we believe every

113

Christian in business should consider before God and, as the Lord directs, make part of his ongoing effort TO ESTABLISH GOD'S KINGDOM ON EARTH." (my emphasis).

Of course that is the bottom line! The idea is to establish the Kingdom on earth … (for example taking item 6) "working towards tax reform, standing for the elimination of graduated income tax, which robs the earner of capital needed to expand business, jobs, capital, etc., and inheritance tax, which injures continuity of ownership and by rightful heirs."

It may be a good objective but is it the Church's role? What are COR's intentions? How far did Jesus Christ trouble Himself with these things? He said *"Render to Caesar the things that are Caesar's, and to God the things that are God's. And they marvelled at Him"* (Mark 12:17).

So however laudable the ideas we do need to exercise discernment right where it's heading.

Christian Reconstruction — The Parallel

Extraordinary New Age nonsense has its parallel in Christian Reconstruction and Kingdom/Dominion Theology, establishing the Kingdom of God. Many are gathering around them teachers who tell them what their itching ears want to hear (2 Timothy 4:3-4). "Another Jesus" (2 Corinthians 11:3-4) is being preached, and that Jesus is the kingdom of self and dominion. In the jargon words , we are the "ongoing incarnation." *"The prophets prophesy falsely, and the priests bear rule by their means; and my people love to have it so"* (Jeremiah 5:31).

The corrupt "Christian" message of hope widely broadcast today is misguided yet subtle, and therefore as dangerous as that of the New Ager. The message is built on a wrong foundation, quite apart from repentance and faith in Jesus Christ; the foundation is the message of a new group of apostles and prophets with new Christian-sounding revelation. They are set not to *evangelise* the lost, but to *christianise* the world. We look later at New Age politicians including Pat Robertson. Our faith must be built only upon Jesus Christ, the Rock, upon His Word which comprises the teachings of the Old Testament prophets and the New Testament apostles. Paul wrote to the Ephesians:

"... ye are no more strangers and foreigners but fellow citizens with the saints, and of the household of God;

And are built upon the foundation of the apostles and prophets, Jesus Christ himself being the chief corner stone"

(Ephesians 2:19-20).

The Kingdom/Dominion, Christian Reconstruction "apostles and prophets" have taken that scripture to themselves, and with that, New Age teaching has been integrated into large areas of the Church today. It is represented in the following summary* :

● WE are the "ongoing incarnation"
● WE will defeat Satan
● WE redeem modern civilization
● WE must have an earthly defeat of Christ's "enemies"
● WE establish the kingdom
● WE give the kingdom over to the Son
● WE must become spotless
● WE - The Bride of Christ - will overcome death
● WE are little gods

We are little gods! Ye shall be as gods! I have collected quotations by well-known professing Christian leaders who stand on this misinterpretation of John 10:34, declaring that God intends us to become gods. Yet it was the serpent's lie:

"For God doth know that in the day ye eat thereof, then your eyes shall be opened, and ye shall be as gods, knowing good and evil" (Genesis 3:5)

It is not only the Eastern religions, cultists and New Agers who take that lie of Satan to be the truth. We live in days when professedly Christian men, leaders, well versed in much that the Bible teaches, are falling for that most deadly lie, the lie that *we* are gods.

---

* *"Report from Concerned Christians"* (P.O. Box 22920, Denver, Colorado 80222) (Vol 8 November/December 1987).

Evangelist Pat Robertson — Candidate for President of the United States

We come now to the American politician with a Christian label, one who is at the same time one of the best known names through Christian television. Robertson's hidden agenda is for a "Secret Kingdom." His book of that name tells us of "eight laws" of the "Secret Kingdom," that are at work behind all genuine happiness. It is the utopian formula of the man who ran well for the Republican Party in 1988, though it wasn't aired in the campaign.

One of his laws is the "Law of Reciprocity" based upon the principle of a man giving what he expects to receive. Like Barbara Marx Hubbard, the New Age Vice Presidential candidate before him and dealing also in the spiritual dimension, Robertson was faced with the problem of those who don't fall into line. It would not be right to say that Robertson is like Hubbard in all his views. However he sees them as "renegades." To Hubbard they are "self-centred humans." In a chapter titled "Renegades Excluded," in "The Secret Kingdom" we are told there will be no need for prisons. With that in mind, what of the renegrades? He tells us, "As the renegade lives (living outside law and decency) so will he receive from the entire society in force. He will be ostracised ...For domestic tranquility, there must be a police force and a system of justice capable of bringing sure and swift punishment upon those who rebel against society."*

The renegade is not the same as the sinner. The renegade is he who will not cooperate with the christianisation of the world; or he is one who is no help with the harmony, unity and peace that the earth and the world is supposed to give.

The sinner may not cooperate either but it is he who by the law, by the grace of God and through evengelism, may recognise the exceeding sinfulness of sin (Romans 7:13). Neither Robertson's laws, nor a christianised world, nor the New Age, are of any help to him.

* "The Secret Kingdom" by Pat Robertson (Bantam Books Inc. New York - 1982). Used by Permission. Thomas Nelson Publishers.

8

The New Age And Rome

We have not travelled this far through our book without
encountering Rome at several points. We know through our
T.V. and newspapers that Rome has a Pope who is
engaging New Agers wherever they meet. We have seen at
the Baca Grande the influence of the Carmelite Roman
Catholic community engaged in a special kind of New Age
ecumenism. Ecumenism with both professing Christians
outside the Roman Catholic faith and with other religions
is taking place across the world. For a global perspective
we find no better example than the gathering at Assisi in
1986.

1986: Two Assisi Events

Events at Assisi in 1986 were reported widely in the
world's press. What does "Assisi - 1986" first bring to
mind?

Pope John Paul II had called for a World Day of Prayer
at Assisi for 27th October 1986. Then, to back that up still
further, on 3rd October 1986, the Pope conceived the idea
of a one-day global truce for that day. And so it came to
pass that while representatives like the Archbishop of
Canterbury prayed, and while the other religious leaders
prayed to their own gods - specifically Budda, Bramha,
Shanti, Vishnu, ancestral spirits, the Great Spirit, Mother
Earth and the Four Winds - warring parties in countries like
Nicaragua, El Salvador and Cambodia, acceded to the

Pope's appeal that combattants lay down their arms for 24 hours on October 27th. Associated Press reported 160 participants at the Prayer Meeting in Assisi represented 32 denominations and groups from Christendom, as well as American Indians, African animists, Japanese Shintoists, Buddhists, Hindus, Sikhs, Jains and Baha'is, with 3.5 billion, or 70% of the world's population, represented there. And, as the A.P. News photograph showed, leaders like John Pretty-on-Top, a Crow Indian, were shaking hands with organiser John Paul II.

Or does "Assisi - 1986" first call to mind a different, and yet no-so-different, event?

The World Wild Life Fund and Rome

Four days before the Pope conceived the idea of the global truce, and just a month before the Pope's gathering, religious leaders were already gathered in Assisi (26th-29th September 1986). This event formed the "launching pad for a permanent alliance between conservation and religion."* It was a World Wildlife Fund (WWF) Event.

Looking over our shoulder do we see Rome again - in her familiar way, supporting movements that will serve her ends with a World religion based on Rome, and now encouraging the Earth Worshippers and animists, the ancient heroes of the New Agers? However we are concerned primarily with the New Age movement and therefore it is *this* WWF "Assisi - 1986" event . we examine. Rome is assuredly interested, but it is this Assisi event, after the style of the Harmonic Convergence described previously, which most involves religion and the Earth (the environment!) The key is its focus, not on the Creator, but on the creation. This undue religious focus goes far beyond proper biblical concern for the environment.

New Age deception often starts, as seen in earlier chapters, with genuine and proper concerns. Apart from a

* "The New Road - the Bulletin of the WWF Network on Conservation and Religion" (Issue No 1 Winter 86/87)

biblical base and apart from the body of true Christian Bible-believers, involvement with groups like Friends of the Earth, Greenpeace, C.N.D., and the World Wildlife Fund (now called the World Wide Fund for Nature) can soon lead to a religious focus upon the creation.

The 25th Anniversary of the World Wildlife Fund was in 1986 and a conservation conference was planned for the occasion. "How did an uncomplicated conservation conference planned for somewhere like Jakarta or New Delhi turn into a multi-faith celebration in the Italian hilltop town of Assisi, with participants ranging from the vice-president of the World Jewish Congress and the secretary of the Muslim World League to a Hindu temple dancer and a Bahai flautist?" The "Radio Times"* (27th September - 3rd October 1986) asked that question and it provided the answer.

"The answer lies with HRH The Duke of Edinburgh, who thought that the World Wildlife Fund's idea of celebrating its 25th anniversary with a scientific and economic congress was stuffy. 'How boring,' commented the President of WWF International, according to one participant, '... Why don't we bring all the religions together? They've all got something to say about conservation, so let's get them to say it and then do something.'

"His enthusiasm had been prompted by a recent reading of 'Worlds of Difference,' a WWF sponsored book written by Martin Palmer and Esther Bisset for use in schools, showing through a retelling of the creation stories from eight religions how our basic attitudes towards the environment are shaped by our beliefs.

"Prince Philip then took the idea a stage further, suggesting Assisi, birthplace of the nature-loving St. Francis (1182-1226), as a possible location, and pilgrimage as a means of getting there..."

"It came to pass. Martin Palmer, the 33-year old co-author of "Worlds of Difference," who heads his own inter-faith educational consultancy ... was brought in to

* "Roger Royle: Good Morning Sunday, 7.30 am Radio 2 "Martin Palmer explains to Steve Turner how the Duke of Edinburgh started it all"

119

develop the pilgrimage ... celebrations designed to establish a new alliance between religion and environmentalism.''

Palmer was expecting "the biggest inter-faith event of its kind ever.'' The flood gates had been opened and, except they escaped, those thousands of members properly concerned for wildlife would risk being washed away with the new religious dimension that was about to dominate the affairs of the WWF.

Prince Philip, President of the WWF, opened the proceedings and "Assisi Declarations" mapping the way from destruction of nature to its conservation were given by the President of the World Jewish Congress, the Secretary General of the Muslim World League, the President of the Virat Hindu Samaj, and the personal representative of His Holiness the Dalai Lama for the Buddhists. Extracts of the Declarations are given in "The New Road."*

What of the so-called "Christian" Declaration? Alas obviously and not surprisingly, the Declaration came from the Roman Catholic Minister General of the Franciscan Order. An event in the birthplace of St. Francis was bound to give credibility to the claims of Rome. Rome was not evidently involved with the WWF initiative at Assisi. Yet when religious seeds are sown we do well to understand that Rome considers herself supreme. She looks for a harvest that will be hers.

The World Wild Life Fund Changes Its Name — And It Changes The Harvest Festival Too!

The World Wildlife Fund changed its name to the wide ranging "Worldwide Fund for Nature". Also, following Assisi, the Harvest Festival, described by the WWF "according to statistics... the third most popular festival after Christmas and Easter," seems set to take a new form.

---

* - the Bulletin of the WWF Network on Conservation and Religion, Issue No 1.

According to the Western, professedly Christian, perspective of WWF-UK "Harvest Festival seemed the natural point in the Church's calendar to stop and consider our faith's insights, revelations and teachings on our role in the created world, and to reconsider our relationship with our fellow creatures."*

The harvest glorifies God. All we do has to glorify Him. The danger with Harvest Festivals always was that they would glorify the creation and man, not God Himself. Yet, as a direct result of Assisi, on Sunday 4th October 1987, Winchester Cathedral was the scene of the first "Creation Harvest Festival." It included a pilgrimage to Winchester (2nd to 4th October) and in the words of WWF, "this walk for nature gave the opportunity for people to meet other Christians and members of other faiths who share their concern for the natural world."*

The need, WWF tell us, is for "a new covenant... At the Winchester celebration we launched the Rainbow Covenant ... between us and God ... us and our neighbour, and us and nature." Christians, beware of a false gospel: "it is designed to be used by schools, churches and other groups to symbolise their commitment to caring for nature."* Symbolic of the pagan blood covenant, itself a corruption and counterfeit of the covenant made by Jesus Christ in His blood, where wrists are cut and joined together, the WWF paper on "Faith and Environment" tells us: "by tying rainbow threads onto each other's wrists we acknowledge our need for each other and to commit ourselves to care for nature. The Rainbow Covenant is designed for all those of goodwill to make. The prayer of covenant, which should be said antiphonally, is as follows, and we invite you to make use of it as you will:

"Brothers and sisters in creation, we covenant this day with you and with all creation yet to be:

With every living creature and all that contains and sustains you;

* "Faith and Environment" (WWF-UK) - a leaflet

121

With all that is on earth and with the earth itself;

With all that lives in the waters and with the waters themselves;

With all that flies in the skies and with the sky itself. We establish this covenant, that all our powers will be used to prevent your destruction.

We confess that it is our own kind who put you at risk of death.

We ask for your trust

and as a symbol of our intention

we mark our covenant with you by the rainbow.

This is the sign of the covenant between ourselves and every living thing that is found on the earth.''

"Creation Harvest Festival" - 1988

Two years after Assisi, one year after Winchester, the WWF wheels continued to turn; the creation story was now rewritten. With a continuing boldness, "The New Road" headline in Issue No 7 (October-December 1988) ran "Church Rewrites Creation Story." This time the "Creation Festival" (as "The New Road" described it) was in Coventry Cathedral and it established "a regular event on the annual Christian calendar ..."

"At the heart of the liturgy devised especially for the service is a revolutionary retelling of the Creation story in the light of evolution ... it weaves the Word of God with the Big Bang, and goes on to detail the succession of creatures which have inhabited our earth - trilobites, graptolites and brachiopods, leading through dinosaurs, fishes and birds to the emergence of Man. Where have they gone, these ancient fearsome beasts? They with the tiny ammonites and belemnites are now extinct. Do we still carry them in our blood? By amazing coincidence, many of these creatures actually lay at our feet in the hundreds of fossils contained in the polished stone paving the cathedral nave.''

"The Provost of Coventry and other ministers present were all happy with what is nothing less than a radical rethinking of the Christian creation story. It takes science on board while retaining the key principles of Genesis.

Another important feature of the liturgy is the Call to Reconciliation with the haunting refrain: 'Father forgive us for we know not what we did.' For the Bishop of Coventry who also attended the service, the notions of sin and repentance are key: 'We have sinned against the environment and the world,' he said, 'and our repentance lies in dedicating ourselves' to preserving the environment. 'Such a redemptive way of living should be part of the Christian task,' added the Bishop.''*

That's a far cry from Luke 15:21, *"And the son said unto him, Father I have sinned against heaven,"* and Psalm 51:4, where David prayed for the remission of sins, *"Against thee, thee only, have I sinned, and done this evil in thy sight."* And Paul didn't testify repentance to anyone but God, "Repentance toward God, and faith toward our Lord Jesus Christ" (Acts 20:21).

The service ended with a New Age ceremony. The photograph in "The New Road" shows Martin Palmer. His book had sparked the Duke of Edinburgh's idea. Now, as Director of International Consultancy on Religion, Education and Culture (ICOREC), he had "played a leading role in devising the liturgy." The photograph shows the tree, "the conservationist's symbol of life," presented by the Director of WWF-UK to the Provost. The Director is shown receiving a "Cross of Nails" from the Provost. They are right, "the cross symbolises the transformation of death into life," yet what confusion these symbols cause when they are not to be found in God's Word. The focus has to be on Jesus Christ, crucified, risen and ascended, and on Him alone. Yet in all these writings we search with difficulty for a single mention of that name which is above every name - JESUS CHRIST.

* "The New Road" No. 7 (October-December 1988)

Five Faiths Become Seven

Five faiths made their declarations at Assisi. "The New Road" tells us that the leaders, now of seven faiths, were invited to address both Houses of Parliament, an "invitation prompted by HRH The Duke of Edinburgh."* "His Royal Highness had drawn the Group's attention to organised religious participation as one of the most significant developments in natural conservation."* Another photograph shows the WWF Director, alongside Martin Palmer, and the leaders now including the Baha'i faith which gave its commitment at Winchester Creation Festival, and the Sikh faith which presented its "initial official statement on conservation for the first time ever that day." "For members of the network it was a time to reaffirm their commitment to conservation two years after its creation at Assisi."

Canterbury Here We Come!

WWF and ICOREC next planned the "Conference on Christian Faith and Ecology" in Canterbury in September 1989. Enter now the British Council of Churches (BCC)! The WWF details tell us, "The BCC, as part of its response to the Justice, Peace and Integrity of Creation process inaugurated by the WCC," is sponsoring the conference jointly with the WWF. "The conference forms part of the Festival of Faith and Environment, the largest ever event in the U.K. linking the major world faiths and environmental organisations... The festival is being organised by the WWF on behalf of the Network on Conservation and Religion, a consortium of representatives from seven faiths and various conservation and environmental bodies."

Leading speakers included senior Roman Catholics and Anglican leaders as well as the Director of Friends of the Earth. The theme of the conference was "Christian Faith

* "The New Road" No. 7 (October-December 1988)

and Ecology,'' a theme recognised not only at Assisi in 1986 but also at a gathering I attended in that year - "Festival '86.''

Festival '86 was quite a different gathering, Christians as opposed to multi-faith, yet where Restoration/Kingdom Now/Dominion Doctrine/Reconstructionist beliefs were predominant, but where also the Director of Friends of the Earth had been invited to speak. Admittedly not a Christian, not making any sort of profession nor speaking from that perspective, the sermon which brought a religious focus upon the earth, earned a good ovation from the congregation. Then the Christian leaders made the tape available. Many roads lead to Rome.

Our concern need not be with the men of Canterbury; we have for long known where the hierarchy of the Church of England stands. The real significance is again that the Canterbury conference presented another opportunity not to glorify God but to lead men to a glorification of the harvest, the environment and the creation. It is the way of our pagan forbears, and, in the words of the Duke of Edinburgh, giving the Dimbleby Lecture*, flying in the face of Scripture (Jeremiah 27:5) and quoting Indians 150 years ago, "Man belongs to the Earth.''

"In the spiritual realm where the battle is (Ephesians 6:12) there is of course more to all this than "Wildlife" or even "Nature" in general. The Duke of Edinburgh has spoken of a "loose association" between the religions and WWF in *The Network of Religion and Conservation,* and that "the network has come to be recognised as a new and potentially very valuable link between the world's religions." The Duke tells us that since much of the sacred literature is not available in any of the principal international languages, there were problems "about the mutual comprehension of the relevant scriptural texts." At this point enter a new body! The International Sacred Literature Trust! The Duke was there, at the United Nations Building in New York, on 22nd May 1989 to launch this Trust. King James gave us the Authorised

* "Living off the Land" (Dimbleby Lecture - BBC Radio)

Version Bible and now we have our Queen's husband launching the Trust and what he calls its "ambitious programme of translation and publication." He believes 'there is a very real possibility that the Sacred Literature Trust will make a significant contribution to inter-faith dialogue.'"*

The Duke had seen to it that Assisi was a significant gathering. Assuredly it was watched carefully by the Vatican, and the Papal Assisi followed a month afterwards. Did we not see at Assisi, Rome's two-fold bid for the religions of the world, not only the recognised ones like the Buddhists and the Hindus, but the American Indians, the pagan people, the New Agers, who set their focus upon the Earth, upon the energy, upon the spirit, within it?

Rome, The New Age and World Religion

The Pope has travelled hundreds of thousands of miles establishing himself as a significant world leader - the potential leader of all the world's religions - and he doesn't leave out the native religions, those who worship the Earth, religions much admired in the Baca Grande, in Boulder, in Glastonbury and in Sedona, Arizona.

The "Arizona Republic" (15th September 1987) had banner headlines: "'Greatest Honour' bestowed on pontiff: Over the last basket woven by his mother, a Pina medicine man blessed an American eagle feather and presented it to an enraptured Pope John Paul II... It was the last basket my mother wove before she passed away seven years ago." In the basket was sand from the Gila Reservation. This represented the earth, she said. "He (the Pope) loved it. When I looked at him, I really felt like there was no one else except him and me. It was a very, very spiritual experience. He took my hand in both of his hands. They felt just kind of real saintly, just strong and firm."

---

* "New Age Bulletin" (Roy and Rae Livesey) No 11, June 1989

Those were the words spoken by a lady on an Indian Reservation south of Phoenix. Then there were those like Patricia from the ecumenical Carmelite Community at the Baca Grande: "We are like the crowd on Palm Sunday who waved branches in great acclaim and later sent Christ to the gallows. We could not tolerate the quality of his presence, believe deeply enough, rise to the challenge of his message … Almost all those who came were touched by a mystic, a man of profound faith constantly at prayer."*

Will we be surprised, in the light of Scripture, if many who beat a path to the Papal door in the Vatican, "touched by a mystic," will also have that "very very spiritual experience"? Isn't that to be expected from the man who claims to be the only Vicar of Christ on earth?

Who else could inspire the airport of a major city to carefully remove a section of apron concrete about 6″ x 8″, and because it was kissed by him, have it displayed in a glass case at the inter-faith chapel? The plaque beneath the stone at London's Gatwick Airport reads:

"This core of concrete removed from the airport apron was the piece of ground kissed by His Holiness Pope John Paul II on landing at Gatwick 08-00 hours on 28th May 1982. This was the historic first visit by a reigning Pope to Great Britain." Then a photograph shows the Pope, hands flat on the concrete, nose hard against the ground as he kissed it.

The Pope visited Britain before he visited the United States, but in America "Our Lady" went before him! In 1985 the London "Daily Telegraph" headlined a "wholly moving experience" at Ballinspittle where Mary's moving statue drew the crowds. Yet that was not Britain, but Ireland where Roman Catholics are not as flippant as the headline! Knock (Ireland), Fatima (Portugal), Medjugorje (Jugoslavia), Lourdes; these are well known. Now Mary is supposed to have manifested her presence in Bayside, New York.

The message from Bayside: "The rosary will be the link

* "Desert Call" (Spring, 1988) Spiritual Life Institute

127

to heaven. All those who ignore our Lady's message will be lost.'' In the counterfeit light generated by the Pope, in a country of millions of New Agers, probably multi-thousands hearing clear voices by which they live their lives, is not the ground being prepared, in both the physical and spiritual realms, to bring more and more into a world religion led by the one whom the Bible calls Antichrist? The Apostle John styles the leader of apostate Christianity, ''that antichrist.'' The ''Vicar of Christ,'' one of the Pope's titles, is ''Antichristos'' in Greek. In English that is Antichrist, which means 'other Christ', rather than against Christ. In other words a different Christ, an unbiblical Christ, is presented and represented.

Global Conferences

There is hardly an important global conference - and these days there are many - that does not have important Roman Catholic involvement, and we look here at one with New Age involvement also; further details are found in ''Understanding the New Age - World Government and World Religion.''*

The Global Survival Conference of Spiritual and Parliamentary Leaders on Human Survival was held at Oxford in 1988. One very senior Roman Catholic, Cardinal Koenig, who has attended similar conferences over many years, including Moral ReArmament ones, was responsible for the inaugural meditation on the theme ''to come together in mutual respect and love.'' Further evidencing the way Rome is both reaching out to other faiths and deceiving unwary Christians, his request was: ''each of you to pray in the language of your tradition and your belief, just as I as a Christian pray to my Father in Heaven.''

Mother Teresa was there and the Report shows a picture of her praying the rosary. Karan Singh, who gave the Assisi Declaration for Hinduism, was also there, and interestingly he tells of what may have been a rehearsal for Oxford, for in the quarterly magazine of Global Forum he writes: ''I was at an Inter Action Council meeting in Rome, where

* New Wine Press, 1989

spiritual and policital leaders debated many of the issues that were faced at Oxford.''

The 14th Dalai Lama told the gathering at Oxford: ''Sometimes I call our planet ''Mother.'' Because of the planet we human beings came into existence.'' The High Priest of the Sacred Forest of Togo was there. However it was left to James Lovelock, a chemist from Reading University, England, to sum up the position for those who favoured earth worship: ''My view of the earth sees a self-sustaining system named Gaia like one of those forest trees.'' And one final quotation from the Report: ''Humanity cannot destroy the earth, but if the goddess Gaia is sufficiently provoked, she can destroy humanity.''

Yet these idolatrous ways of regarding the earth and the goddess Gaia surely have no more power to do good and evil than the idols mentioned in Jeremiah 10:3-5, *''Be not afraid of them; for they cannot do evil, neither also is it in them to do good.''*

In the Global Forum newsletter I read that Moscow will host the next Conference in 1990. Three ''Christianity'' members of the Global Forum Council are listed - one Metropolitan, one Cardinal (Koenig again), and the New Age leader, the Very Rev. James Parks Morton of the Cathedral of St John the Divine in Manhattan, the cathedral housing the headquarters of Lindisfarne which has a Centre at the Baca Grande, looked at in chapter four. There is no lack of evidence of Rome's enthusiasm in cooperating with the New Age. Indeed it must be reckoned that she has a good measure - an increasing measure - of influence and control.

Christian author, Joseph Carr in ''The Lucifer Connection'' suggests that One World Religion is ''the bottom line of the New Age.'' Is that correct? The New Age IS a religion and New Agers are uniting. The religious are uniting. Yet don't we find in the writings of Carr and others, all seeking to expose the New Age from a Christian perspective, too little recognition given to the role of Rome in establishing that one-world religion?

I believe that when we recognise the New Age and

understand it for what it is (and its presence is very clear to those who have eyes to see), we still need to keep close to God's Word. What is the papacy? Who is "that antichrist"? Were all those great Christian men over nineteen centuries not right who saw the papacy as "that antichrist" of 1 John 2:18? Has Rome really changed? Isn't it just the strategy which has changed?

We see the New Age movement. It is very real. Yet it needs exposing, and Christian writers have done a useful work. Don't we see through the pages of history, right back to Babylon, and even through the few recent events summarised in this book, that something much bigger than the Western civilisation's New Age movement is being united together? Is it surprising that the system that for more than a thousand years has laid claim to the souls of men and produced a dynasty of "Vicars of Christ" would be involved in the action? Should we not therefore look further than the New Age movement and the Eastern and pagan religions which it follows, to find the source? Do we find Rome?

"And upon her forehead was a name written, MYSTERY, BABYLON THE GREAT, THE MOTHER OF HARLOTS AND ABOMINATIONS OF THE EARTH" (Revelation 17:5).

Rome And The New Age — Both From Babylon

Had the religious ones in Babylon not heard of the one who we know as Jesus? Did God not say that he would *"put enmity between thee and the woman, and between thy seed and her seed; it shall bruise thy head, and thou shalt bruise his heel"* (Genesis 3:15)? That scripture speaks of Jesus who was to be born of a virgin by the Holy Spirit. Nimrod built Babylon but there came his wife, Semiramis, claiming after Nimrod's death the virgin birth of a reincarnated Nimrod, her child Tammuz. There was the counterfeit, the mother and child transferred to Mary and the Babylonian counterfeit of Jesus.

With the scattering from Babel encouraged by the babble of the different languages God caused to come upon them, many different branches of the same antichrist religion were formed and we see them holding on to the worship, not directly of Nimrod, but of the second and third persons of this unholy trinity, the mother and child. Now with different languages they had different names.

The Chinese had a mother goddess called Shingmoo or the "Holy Mother." The ancient Germans worshipped the virgin Hertha with child in arms. The Scandinavians called her Disa who was pictured with a child. The Etruscans called her Nutria. The Virgo-Patitura was worshipped as the "Mother of God" among the Druids. In India she was Indrani, represented with child in arms. To the Greeks the mother goddess was Aphrodite or Ceres. She was Nana to the Sumerians. More familiar, we may know Venus and her child Jupiter in Rome. We have mother and child, Devaki and Crishna, and again in India we have Isi and Iswara. In Asia there was (and of course everywhere there still is!) mother and child worship; the mother was Cybele and the child was Deoiüs. Really all these mythical women were the wives of Nimrod, later the wives of Baal.

The true God gives life. This counterfeit Babylonian god is the supposed father of Tammuz born long after Nimrod's death. He became Baal in Egypt, represented by the phallus, the male organ of reproduction which is the giver of life. As we look at the obelisk in St. Peters Square in Rome what we see is the symbol of a phallus, of Baal. In pagan religion we find a complex of beliefs often involving mother and child, fertility and sexual connotations. The other giver of life is seen, again with some credibility, necessary for the creation and for life on earth, the sun. The Vatican obelisk was brought from Egypt in 1586 up to which time it stood for sun worship.

When the children of Israel fell into apostasy we read in the Bible what transpired: *"And they forsook the Lord, and served Baal and Ashtaroth"* (Judges 2:13). The Israelites were into the apostasy that the Church is into today. Just like those Christians today who draw increasingly fast towards Rome, here were a people who had known the leading of the true God now worshipping the mother Ashtaroth. One of the titles by which she was known to the Israelites was the "queen of heaven." If we haven't already recognised in the scenario above the roots of the counterfeit Mary and Jesus of the Roman Catholic counterfeit church, Jeremiah's description of this "queen of heaven" worshipped by the children of Israel, and his warning (Jeremiah 44:17-19), ought to drive home the relevance of all this. The "queen of heaven" is a Roman Catholic title.

Babylon - Egypt - Rome

We come now to Egypt. The mother was Isis and the child was Horus. Then eventually, all this false worship having spread from Babylon to the various nations, in different names and forms, it came to Rome. The classic study in magic and religion, *"The Golden Bough"* by Sir James Frazer, tells us that the worship of the Great Mother was "very popular" under the Roman Empire, and he quotes particularly those provinces of Rome (Italy, Spain, Portugal, France etc) which are of course strong in Roman Catholicism today. It was during this period when the worship of the mother was prominent, that the Saviour of mankind, Jesus Christ, was born to Mary. Unlike Semiramis, Mary was not one deceived. Assuredly she knew herself to be an ordinary woman. We know from the Bible that He was born in Bethlehem, truly of a Virgin, but by One who put enmity between the Devil and the Woman (Genesis 3:15). He was conceived by the Holy Spirit. This was not a reincarnation as Semiramis regarded Tammuz, and as New Agers today would have it. Furthermore it was not the Woman (Mary) who "shall crush" the serpent's head as the Roman Catholic Rheims-Douay Bible would have it in Genesis 3:15.

Let us not mistake from whence this Mother and Baby-Jesus idolatry comes. By the time of Constantine in the fourth century, Mary was looked upon as a goddess. In the fifth century at the Council of Ephesus, in the place where

Diana, the goddess of Virginity and motherhood was worshipped and where the Temple of Diana was one of the seven wonders of the world, Mary worship was made OFFICIAL Roman Catholic doctrine.

Don't we need to cast out all that is pagan lest it gets a hold on us? Wasn't it understandable that those at Ephesus would bring the character of their goddess with them? We can comprehend it. We can see that these were not truly saved. The Holy Spirit is the One who leads into all truth, and the mother and child religions, the religions from the scattered Babylon, found their ready focus in Rome. There had been made a clear and timely assault on the credibility of the one who was born to save us from our sins. John wrote that *"even now there are many antichrists"* and he warned *"that antichrist shall come"* (1 John 2:18). In referring to "antichrist", the one that "shall come", wasn't John referring, not to the variety of god-mother-child trinities that followed Nimrod, Semiramis and Tammuz', the "many antichrists" that existed in John's day, but to THE antichrist, seen by the coming together of the Babylon religions into the Roman Catholic and eventually the papal system? Doesn't the root from John Paul II in our own day trace easily back to Babylon?

The occultic and materialistic focus on the creation we see in the New Age movement has been with us since the scattering from Babylon. The Roman Empire eventually took its pick of what it wanted from the pagan religions by then dispersed around the world. Then out of the multitude of Roman gods came the variety of Roman Catholic saints. The ecumenical Roman Catholics are encouraged by their leaders to pray to them today. In the July/August 1987 Roman Catholic magazine "New Covenant"* we read of "a modern girl" discovering "real beauty" and praying and asking the intercession of St. Bridget that she might realise how false is the worship of beauty.

What we today know as Eastern Religion (summed up in Hinduism) and the New Age, with the same supposed communication with the dead - with deceiving spirits - goes

* an American monthly magazine

back beyond Rome to Babylon itself. Rome has carried the flag, a counterfeit christianity, for more than a thousand years. Now, preparing to pass as the only church in the eyes of many in the Church today, it is poised also for ecumenical unity with New Agers, with ecology groups and the occultists, also with the rest of Satan's religious deceptions.

The New Age has entered the Church.* Rome is wooing the New Age. What of Christians who have taken New Age teaching on board? Deceived already, these are among the many who have leaders beating a path to the papal door.

Pope — "Prince of Peace Award" or Antichrist?

The apostasy described in 2 Thessalonians 2:1-12 and 1 Timothy 4:1-3 seems to refer to no ordinary falling away such as known to churches since Pentecost. In Brown's *"Structure of the Apocalypse"*** THE Apostasy is described: It was to be such an outbreak of clerical ambition that was well nigh impossible when Christians were a persecuted people. It supposes the Church an organised body and its ministers able to mount to heights almost incredible. I don't know if the last Pope will be THE Antichrist, but in the words of Richard Baxter who ministered in Kidderminster, the town of my birth, in the seventeenth century, "If the pope be not Anti-Christ he hath ill-luck to be so like him!" Rome does not change; it is its strategy that changes. Since Pope John XXIII the strategy has been to go out and win converts to Rome. Rome does this today not through opposition and inquisition.

One leader, introduced in *UNDERSTANDING DECEPTION,* is Harold Bredesen, a man very well known in the United States. He helped promote Pat Robertson, the recent presidential candidate who believed God had

---

* - for further reading on this subject "Understanding Deception - New Age Teaching in the Church" by Roy Livesey (New Wine Press, 1987) covers a broad spectrum of deception in the charismatic/ecumenical church.

** Quoted in "FOCUS - Facts and Comment on the Current Religious Scene" (Sept/Oct 1988) "Focus", 6 Orchard Road, Lewes, East Sussex BN7 2HB

appointed him a modern John the Baptist, and who is set to get the first television shots of Christ's return to earth. The prophecy that God chose Christian Broadcasting Network and Pat Robertson to "usher in the coming of my Son" came through the man who is important here, Harold Bredesen.

Some Christian leaders prophesied that Anwar Sadat was a possible candidate for Antichrist. Sadat was a peacemaker after the style of some, even Gorbachev, who are receiving the plaudits today. Christians are heard to be encouraged by Gorbachev's deceptions. Bredesen promoted Sadat and so presented him favourably, and in 1980 in Washington D.C., in company which included the Chaplain of the United States Senate and Pat Robertson, Sadat was presented with the award that Bredesen founded: "The Prince of Peace Award." That is amazing since it is our Lord who is Wonderful, Counsellor, The Mighty God, The everlasting Father, THE PRINCE OF PEACE (Isaiah 9:6).

A decade later *"Take Heed Update"** reports that a proposal for the "Prince of Peace Prize and Festival" reads: "The choice of recipient is obvious. A growing worldwide consensus of Christians and non-Christians see Pope John Paul II as the great peace maker of our day - the man who can most effectively focus the eyes of the world on peace and its true source." I didn't sense that the deception of Christians was so far gone, but the organisers of this Papal Award are well-networked with others, and if nothing else they should be well-informed. So in their statement they are probably right. Certainly, and because this is THE apostasy, there are many Christians who do see the Pope bringing peace in this way.

New leaders who have joined the original 1980 committee to prepare for the big 1990 event include Father Tom Forrest, head of Rome's decade of evangelism known as "Evangelisation 2000." The plan to bring forward both a one-world religion and a one-world government is reinforced by apostate Christians at various points. Also there is overlap between these powerful religious forces

* Concerned Christians, P.O. Box 22920, Denver, CO 80222, USA (Sept/Oct 1988)

and those more-or-less-hidden, behind-the-scenes forces who represent world government, at least in the measure we have it today. The important name of Armand Hammer crops up in several places. The name of Hammer crops up now! He was there in the U.S. with his aides in a suite adjacent to the Gorbachev aides on the Russian leader's recent "peace" visit to the U.S. Can Hammer now help tie in Gorbachev to this "Christian" initiative which is still in its planning stages?

Heads of State and ambassadors are expected to participate at the 1990 Rome event and it is hoped that Gorbachev and Reagan will participate. Mrs Sadat has requested that Reagan do the honours of officially presenting the award. As for help in opening the doors to Gorbachev, the leaders have briefly elaborated on their meeting with the Hollywood producer of the film *"Ben Hur."* This producer is a friend of Occidental Petroleum Chairman, Armand Hammer, and he is doing a movie of Hammer's life in Russia. Bredesen told the producer, "God gave me a vision to go and talk to Gorbachev. Would you talk to Armand Hammer and help us get there?

I believe the point is well made here that it matters little on the human view whether or not Mr. Hammer can help. It matters not, except the Lord wills, whether or not this leader or that leader attends the festivities of 1990 in Rome. Our purpose is simply to relate some of the things that may help readers discern the signs of the times, and indeed discern THE Apostasy about which the Bible speaks.

We have noted Gerry Falwell and "Reverend" Moon. Now it's "Ben Hur", and Armand Hammer, and Harold Bredesen, and Gorbachev! What a mess! Christians in Britain and around the world do have to take care with the leadership and teaching that comes from the United States.

The New Age is in vogue, but its root goes back to Babylon. If it is right, as I believe it to be, that the Church of Rome is the Babylon of Revelation 17, then is it not right to watch Rome and warn those who will involve themselves with her? When men like Hudson Taylor, Moody, Spurgeon, Jonathan Edwards, Toplady, Wesley, John

136

Bunyon, Richard Baxter, Ridley, Latimer, Luther and Wycliffe, believed Rome to be the Babylon of Revelation 17, and the popes to be that antichrist prophesied in Scripture, then are we not right to be cautious and watch what Rome is doing? Believers need far more discernment in such matters.

9

Christians, The New Age and New Agers

A study of the New Age is in one sense like a study of Scripture. The more that is revealed, the more obvious it becomes that there is so much more. We are not to follow that path into the depths of the New Age. It is a path which invites deception. To discern the New Age is quite a different matter. Our discernment comes from an awareness from Scripture of Satan's devices.

A Time for Watchmen

It is always a time for watchmen! Certainly it is such a time today. Where then does this place the Christian? We certainly do not major on what the New Agers tell us. However when this confirms what the Bible says then we do well to reckon the activities of the New Age as a sign of these times. As for ourselves, we are in Satan's sights too. Let us test everything against the Word of God and beware of the theories and teaching of men. We are seeing signs and wonders. Let us discern what is from God; let us discern the teaching that comes from God. In the beginning was the Word (John 1:1) and the Word became flesh (John 1:14). When we keep our eyes upon Jesus Christ, including what He says about Satan, we shall know Him and His Word. Like Ezekiel we can be watchmen and warn those brothers and sisters in Christ who are going astray:

"Son of man. I have made thee a watchman unto the house of Israel: therefore hear the word at my mouth, and give them warning from me" (Ezekiel 3:17).

"If when he seeth the sword come upon the land, he blow the trumpet, and warn the people; Then whosoever heareth

the sound of the trumpet, and taketh not warning; if the sword
come, and take him away, his blood shall be upon his own
head'' (Ezekiel 33:3-4).

New Age Beliefs or The Bible?

We see a wide spectrum of New Age beliefs. When we look
at what New Agers believe, we may spot inconsistencies and
areas where New Agers take opposite views. We need
concern ourselves little with their differences; what we need
to know is that our witness to New Agers amounts to an
offensive in the spiritual realm. Our witness will be effective
only as the Holy Spirit brings the light, so that these deluded
people may hear the Gospel message.

I believe the apparent hotch-potch of New Age beliefs can
be recognised as following a pattern. We can discern that
they come from the same spirit - a counterfeit spirit. The
counterfeit spirit leads New Agers to a "package" of
counterfeit belief.

In Old Testament times we read much about the work of
the Spirit of God, starting with Genesis 1:2 when the *"Spirit*
of God moved upon the face of the waters.'' Later in Genesis
we find Pharaoh recognising Joseph as *"a man in whom the*
Spirit of God is'' (Genesis 41:38). We find both Jesus Christ
and the Holy Spirit in every book of the Old Testamant.
Genesis portrays Jesus Christ as our Creator God. Exodus
portrays Him as our Passover Lamb. Leviticus portrays Him
as our Sacrifice for Sin, and so on. There was no written
Bible for Pharaoh and Joseph, yet we are told that even
Pharaoh recognised a man led by the Spirit of God. Are we,
New Testament Christians, recognised as people led by the
Spirit of God?

That is a challenge to us all, but we are concerned here
with the New Age and with New Agers. We can be quite
certain that Joseph, quickened by the Spirit of God, discerned
the spirit at work in Pharaoh. He wasn't blinded by the
esteem heaped upon him nor by Pharaoh's patronage. It was
not a matter of the written word for none existed on either
side. Rather it was a matter of a different spirit. The
difference was in the spiritual realm.

Today we have the advantage, through the sacrifice and shed blood of Jesus Christ, of a New Testament and a written Word of God. In Old Testament times the Saviour was known to those chosen by God; it was known there would be one Jesus who would *"put enmity between thee and the woman, and between thy seed and her seed; it shall bruise thy head, and thou shalt bruise his heel"* (Genesis 3:15). These things could be known by the Spirit.

Today we have the further advantage that through the written Word of God we are able by the Holy Spirit to discern that which is not of God. We can discern New Age activity. Also we do well to keep in mind that New Agers themselves, unlike the atheists or humanists, listen to the spirit - the counterfeit spirit that is in opposition to God.

Following the example of Paul, when *"his spirit was stirred in him, when he saw the city wholly given to idolatry"* (Acts 17:16), we are to "dispute" with New Agers about this New Age spirituality when we are prompted to do so.

The Christian and New Age World Views Compared

God is the Creator; He is personal and He upholds all things with His power. To the New Ager, God is in everyone and in everything. I think of the seance I attended as a New Ager when the medium told me she was "at one with that vase." New Age man is one with all things.

The New Age man is the product of 'evolution', but it is not the "chance" of the humanist or atheist. Man is, to the advanced New Ager, the result of both a physical and spiritual evolution. We are said to be still evolving spiritually, and occasions like the "Harmonic Convergence" and the "World Instant of Cooperation" reflected the hope New Agers have of seeing the "quantum leap" or "paradigm shift" for mankind. They want to bring about the move from the Piscean Age and into the Age of Aquarius, away from the Second Wave of the so-called corrupt industrial society, into the Third Wave where men operating at a new higher

141

level of consciousness (so-called right brain men rather than left-brain men,) would be directing our society.

The Bible tells us that man was created in God's image (Genesis 1:26-27); our guide is God's word (Psalm 119:105; John 20:31; 2 Timothy 3:15-17). The guide for New Age man comes from a spurious mixture of pseudo-science and religion. His "truth" comes by revelation "from within." He does not heed the Lord's warning and the list of evil things that He gives and which all come *"from within, and defile the man"* (Mark 7:21-23). After all the essence of the New Age doctrine is that we are gods! At first it may be reckoned the New Ager's "hunch" as he manages to throw off what he calls left-brain logic. Then later he is rejoicing as he hears more clearly with answers to all his questions; they may come clearly "from within" or they may be by an audible voice. He is deceived into believing in his contact in "the spirit world"; or perhaps his own consciousness has made contact with the "collective consciousness." However he views it, it is all deception. Satan doesn't deal with each man in the same way just as God doesn't deal with all His people in exactly the same way.

The New Ager doesn't know that truth is unchangeable and that we can know right from wrong (Romans 1:32; 2:15). He has no conception of sin, through a failure to follow God. To him human problems are the result of man's separation from the collective consciousness, from the creative or collective being, from each other and from nature. Yet the answer isn't the human knowledge (Isaiah 40:24-25; 1 Corinthians 3:19-20), education, human reason of the humanist. The answer isn't to reach a higher level of consciousness or an at-one-ment. The answer is to fall on the mercy of God (Romans 9:16), to cry out for His forgiveness (Luke 18:13), and to walk obediently (Luke 6: 46-49; John 8:31) according to the ways of Jesus Christ empowered by the Holy Spirit (Romans 8: 1-6).

Language is a problem dealing with the New Ager. Unlike the atheist, he has concepts of God and Christ. Christ is not just a myth. Christ is represented in individuals like Jesus, like Krishna, evolved to a higher plane. Jesus, they say, spent the "missing eighteen years" in India in order that he could prepare himself and reach the higher plane before beginning his main work. Jesus Christ, to the New Ager, is not God Himself, fully God as the Bible teaches. To them He is not the only Saviour and Lord.

The New Ager's experience is his reality. Those who advance in New Age ways, like the lady who was "at one with the vase," know a deceptive spiritual experience more real to them than that known through the physical senses. In a similar way, for the Christian, the walk with an unseen Jesus Christ is truly real (John 14:21). For the Christian, death is not to be feared. Rather we are told only to fear God (Ecclesiastes 12:13), the one whom we shall meet face to face (Job 19:26-27; 1 John 3:2; Revelation 20:12; 22:4). Yet the New Ager has no fear of death either. For him death does not mean a continuing existence where his spirit will live forever, either with the Lord, or for ever separated from Him in hell. To the advanced New Ager, as maybe for the Hindus in their squalour as they suffer day and night on the pavements of cities like Calcutta, death is only an illusion ('maya'). It heralds the passage into another incarnation, another life where the process of karma will bring its natural compensations as we evolve on the pathway to godhood.

Reaching the New Ager with the Gospel

We are concerned with individual New Agers. The Bible allows no opportunity for us to change the ultimate direction the world is headed (2 Peter 3:10); events come to pass according to His Word. We are not to be concerned with 'christianising' the world but with evangelising the lost. The Bible is quite clear that *"straight is the gate, and narrow is the way, which leadeth unto life, and few there be that find it"* (Matthew 7:14). The Bible is quite clear on the other hand that "many" will take the way that leads to destruction (vs 13). Nevertheless we are to evangelise the New Agers and, as for all men, as many as are *"ordained to eternal life"* (Acts 13:48) will believe.

I am sure it is important that church leaders understand the New Age movement, and although I have warned about the New Age, my experience extending over the past seven years has been that they do not. Leaders generally show little understanding of what it's like to be a New Ager. Do most understand if a man, perhaps even in his congregation, speaks of having to leave his body to get some relaxation? Or do they reply "Nonsense!"? Maybe he still is himself unhappily a deceived leader, making his decisions after listening to audible voices in his ear. Does a minister even readily believe a man, again perhaps arrived in his church for counsel and help, troubled by voices he is hearing? Or, once again, is the minister completely non-plussed? Do most ministers understand that Satan is working extraordinary miracles in spiritual and psychic healing circles, miracles of physical healing that have an enormous price tag in the spiritual realm, where most have little or no discernment? Not recognising Satan who masquerades as an angel of light (2 Corinthians 11:14), when they have "proof" of the healing, do they then conclude the healing must be from God?

The fact is that the New Age comes into the churches, into healing meetings and all the fringe groups, because leaders do not discern the New Age. The purpose in writing about the New Age is to encourage leaders and believers with that discernment. Thus the first thing that is helpful when evangelising New Agers is to have some understanding of what they believe. The difficulty of how to deal with a Jehovahs Witness at the door is all too well known. Given that we have the truth of God's word, the Gospel, and given that we know what the J.W. believes, then, led by the Holy Spirit, we are well equipped. It is the same when meeting the New Ager.

First, we are aware of where he stands and where the New Age leads people. Second, we are able to evangelise. Third, we are equipped to dispute with them like Paul in the synagogue at Athens with the Jews (Acts 17:17). Finally, we do well to be versed in the whole counsel of God, in sound doctrine, for in dealing with New Agers we are for the most part, and more and more, dealing with spiritual people.

New Agers are neither humanists nor atheists. Rather they are people who, like me, discovered the spiritual dimension in the realm of the counterfeit. Just like I was, many are searching. Let us approach them with a confidence through knowing that it is God's will that they be saved (1 Timothy 2:4; 2 Peter 3:9), and with an assurance that comes from the knowledge that we offer them spiritual truth to replace spiritual counterfeit - the truth that is found only through repentance for sin by the grace of God, and through faith in the shed blood of Jesus Christ (Romans 3:24-25; Ephesians 2:8-9).

We pray for the New Ager. We pray that he might respond to God's Word. Let us acknowledge what is God's Word and God's work. *"With him is strength and wisdom: the deceived and the deceiver are his"* (Job 12:16). It is God's work to save them. Whilst not overlooking our own role, we do need to be clear on that and note the scriptures: John 6:44; Romans 8:29-30; 1 Corinthians 3:6-9; Philippians 2: 13; 2 Timothy 2:25.

The Bible and The Gospel

New Agers make the common mistake of taking what they will from their experience, from fables, and from those around them who profess to be teachers. Many who profess as Christians can also be found drawing from these sources. They are impressed by their experiences and encouraged by coincidences. Or, as with the "Creation Harvest Festival" liturgy launched at Coventry Cathedral in 1988 where the Genesis story is integrated with the "big bang" view of creation, they select from Scripture, from experience, and from their teachers.

The Holy Spirit must be our teacher (1 Corinthians 2: 12-16); *"Open thou mine eyes, that I may behold wondrous things out of thy law"* (Psalm 119:18). The Bible is clear that teachers are important but it tells us also we have to take care and check what is taught with Scripture just as the Bereans checked what Paul taught (Acts 17:11). The Bible is capable of an infinite number of interpretations, and these are not necessarily what the Holy Spirit teaches. When we are saved we receive the Holy Spirit (Romans 8:14). All true

145

sons *"are led by the Spirit of God"* (Romans 8:14); those who have not received the Spirit are lost (Romans 8:9).

The Bible tells us, *"God created man in his own image, in the image of God created he him; male and female created he them"* (Genesis 1:27). God blessed them and gave them dominion over every living thing. God took the man into the Garden of Eden and there was one thing he was forbidden to do.

God is the Creator and He made just one rule; he was forbidden to eat of the tree of knowledge (Genesis 2:17).

Man was told that if he ate of the tree of knowledge he would "surely die." God had given man the tree of life, but if he ate from the tree of knowledge that would be disobedience. Most important, this meant that man would die spiritually and there would be no eternal life, except separated from God who created him.

Whilst there was no sense, and little future, for man to argue with God who created him (Job 40:1-2), and who could destroy him just as easily, the problem was that God has also created a perfect angelic being called Lucifer (Ezekiel 28:15) who had rebelled in heaven and been cast down to earth (Isaiah 14:12-16). He had been cast out from heaven for challenging God's authority, and he took to himself the body of the serpent (Revelation 12:9).

The serpent challenged the woman by diverting her attention from exactly what God has said, getting her to focus instead on her experience. The fruit looked good to eat (Genesis 3:1-6), and we note the serpent's lie when he said *"For God doth know that in the day ye eat thereof, then your eyes shall be opened, and ye shall be as gods, knowing good and evil"* (vs 5). This must surely be Satan's chief work today - spreading false doctrine (2 Corinthians 11:3).

Eve believed the lie. She took the fruit. Adam followed. Man had fallen. He became separated from God by his sin. His sin was his disobedience, not a small thing in God's sight, and who are we to question God, the Creator (Romans 9:20)? Adam was perfect before he fell, finding favour with God by his own righteousness. When he fell he was no longer a perfect moral being totally obedient to God. He was corrupted. He was "naked" without righteousness. Man had believed Satan's lie when he said *"ye shall be as gods."* Man had died spiritually at the Fall and the position today is that he needs to be born again. This was made possible by Jesus Christ, known all through the Old Testament, and who was to come in the flesh 4,000 years after Adam.

Since the Fall, natural man has known no other way except to live according to his own will (Romans 8:7). *"We have turned every one to his own way"* (Isaiah 53:6). To live according to our own will is quite natural except we receive the Holy Spirit of God, becoming born again of that Spirit. Mostly natural men don't actually say they are "as gods", but that is the effect of what they see as their own will exercised in their lives. When we are born again, we fail so often through indwelling sin (Romans 7:22-25). Though we now hate sin, we can say for sure that we have life, a new spiritual and eternal life. It's not we who live but Christ who lives in us. (Galatians 2:20).

In these days of extreme occultism we find New Agers on the other route - the religious route, not the Christian one - committed to the lie that they can be "as gods." They earnestly strive for spiritual power. They give place to a power that is the counterfeit of the Holy Spirit. Yet all are lost and stand condemned except their sin is dealt with; all men are sinners whether they have been involved in occult sin or not (Ecclesiastes 7:20). Jesus Christ said that *"except a man be born again, he cannot see the kingdom of God"* (John 3:3). The only difference between the New Ager and the kindly old lady, not knowing she was born a sinner, called a sinner in the Bible, and with her own righteousness described as "filthy garments" (Zechariah 3:3-4), is that the New Ager is on the road of counterfeit spiritual experience. God's grace, a true repentance for sin, is the only answer for the New Ager, for the murderer, for the young man, and for the kindly old lady who thinks she will get to Heaven if she does her best. (Isaiah 45:22; 55:6-7).

This salvation which is the need of all men is a salvation from sin (Matthew 1:21). We can have that because Jesus, the Creator of the world, came to live and to die to pay the price of our sin (John 3:16; 1 Corinthians 15:3-4). The wonder of His love cannot be grasped except by faith, but when, by the grace of God, we take that step of faith, we can know His regenerating power (Romans 10:9-10). We are given a new heart. It is a heart that hates sin (Romans 7:15). It is a heart for Jesus Christ and His Word.

The Bible is that Word (Isaiah 55:11). The Word becomes a living Word when the Holy Spirit gives life (1 Peter 1:23). Speaking of Jesus, John tells us *"the Word was made flesh and dwelt among us"* (John 1:14), and back to the creation, the apostle tells us, *"In the beginning was the Word, and the Word was with God, and the Word was God"* (John 1:1). Jesus is God, He was God, and He was also with God in the beginning. *"All things were made by him; and without him was not anything made that was made"* (vs 3).

Jesus Christ came that those who will believe and make Him Lord and Saviour of their lives might be born again (John 3:3). He says He is the only way to eternal life. Does the clay have any right to talk back to the potter? (Romans 9:21). God is the Creator. The Creator commands men to repent (Acts 17:24-31). The Bible says that Jesus Christ is the only way to God. Jesus is the Word. We were created for His glory. Who will dare to argue? God is a God of love (1 John 4:8-9), but He is a just God, and He is everything He says He is.

"O Lord, thou are my God; I will exalt thee, I will praise thy name; for thou hast done wonderful things; thy counsels of old are faithfulness and truth" (Isaiah 25:1). The Bible contains much warning for New Agers and the unsaved. We are to exercise discernment and be the salt and light Jesus told us to be. Satan seeks to deceive even the best of God. I pray that with more discernment you will now be more able to lead New Agers to the one who is able to set them free.

INDEX

152

More books on
The New Age Movement

"Understanding The New Age - World Government and World Religion"
by Roy Livesey (New Wine Press - 1989) 224 pages £3.50
- a **Different** book on "that antichrist", Rome and the Jesuits
- a **Different** look at the Bankers, Credit and the "Love of Money"
- a **Different** perspective on Conspiracy. Wasn't History planned?

"Understanding Alternative Medicine - Holistic Health in the New Age"
by Roy Livesey (New Wine Press - 1988) 224 pages £2.95
- a Christian Perspective on New Age Health Care
- an exposé of the occult in Alternative Medicine
- encouraging Discernment amongst Christians

"Understanding Deception - New Age teaching in the Church"
by Roy Livesey (New Wine Press - 1987) 256 pages £2.95
- highlighting Deception in the Church
- encouraging Christians to check the current Winds of Doctrine
- warning Christians against building an Earthly Kingdom

"The Prince and The Paranormal - The Psyc
bloodline of the Royal Family"
by John Dale (1987) 256 pages £3.50
   following the "search" of Prince Charles in the New
   a Review of long Royal involvement in the Paranor
   evidences the need to Pray for our Rulers

"New Age to New Birth - A personal testim
of two Kingdoms"
by Roy and Rae Livesey (New Wine Press - 1986) 190 p
£2.50
- experiences in the New Age and the Occult
- unravelling Satan's Deceptions as a Christian
   cautionary addendum (1989): measuring Experiences
- Testimony against the Word of God.

Roy and Rae Livesey also publish **New Age Bulletin**

Personal Orders for the above books, and details of **New Age Bulletin**
be supplied to those who write to Roy and Rae Livesey at Bury H
Clows Top, Kidderminster, Worcs. DY14 9HX. England. Add 10%
U.K. postage.